D0046126

# THE LITTLE ROCK SCHOOL DESEGREGATION CRISIS IN AMERICAN HISTORY

# The IN AMERICAN HISTORY Series

IN
AMERICAN
HISTORY

# THE LITTLE ROCK SCHOOL DESEGREGATION CRISIS IN AMERICAN HISTORY

Robert Somerlott

**Enslow Publishers, Inc.**

| | |
|---|---|
| 40 Industrial Road | PO Box 38 |
| Box 398 | Aldershot |
| Berkeley Heights, NJ 07922 | Hants GU12 6BP |
| USA | UK |

http://www.enslow.com

**Library of Congress Cataloging-in-Publication Data**

Somerlott, Robert.
    The Little Rock school desegregation crisis in American history /
Robert Somerlott.
        p. cm. — (In American history)
    Includes bibliographical references and index.
    ISBN 0-7660-1298-0
    1.  School integration—Arkansas—Little Rock—History—20th century.
2.  Afro-American students—Arkansas—Little Rock—History—20th
century. 3.  Afro-Americans—Civil rights—Arkansas—Little Rock—
History—20th century. 4.  Central High School (Little Rock, Ark.)—
History—20th century. 5.  Little Rock (Ark.)—Race relations.  I. Title.
II. Series.
    LC214.23.L56 S66    2001
    373.767'73—dc21

                                                    00-011444

Printed in the United States of America

10 9 8 7 6 5 4 3 2 1

**To Our Readers:** We have done our best to make sure all Internet addresses in
this book were active and appropriate when we went to press. However, the
author and the publisher have no control over and assume no liability for the
material available on those Internet sites or on other Web sites they may link to.
Any comments or suggestions can be sent by e-mail to comments@enslow.com or
to the address on the back cover.

**Illustration Credits:** Betsy Blass, pp. 16, 37, 63, 94, 105, 108, 109;
Cartoon by George Fisher, pp. 48, 101; Enslow Publishers, Inc., p. 17;
Library of Congress, pp. 22, 24, 40, 52, 76; National Archives, pp. 82,
103; Photograph by Janet W. Smith, p. 110; Photograph by Will
Counts, pp. 10, 12, 13, 28, 41, 45, 50, 56, 61, 68, 69, 90, 92, 96;
Reproduced from the *Dictionary of American Portraits*, Published by
Dover Publications, Inc., in 1967, p. 59.

**Cover Illustration:** Library of Congress; Photograph by Will Counts.

# ★ CONTENTS ★

# ELIZABETH ECKFORD ARRIVES AT SCHOOL

On the night of September 4, 1957, Elizabeth Eckford, a fifteen-year-old African-American girl in Little Rock, Arkansas, was worried. Tomorrow was to be her first day at Central High School. She had walked past the big, impressive building several times and knew that the people of Little Rock were proud of the handsome structure. "The finest in the state," they often said.[1] Certainly, Central High School was far bigger and better-equipped than Dunbar High School, the all-black institution where Elizabeth had completed her first two years of high school.

She had never been inside Central High, of course. No African American had ever stepped through its doors as a student. Like practically all schools in the South, Central was strictly segregated by race. "Whites only" was the rule.

That was supposed to change tomorrow. Elizabeth and eight of her African-American schoolmates from Dunbar expected to enroll at Central High in the morning.

This change in the whites-only system had come about because of an order from the United States Supreme Court. The segregated public school system, described as "separate but equal" had been declared unlawful. Separate, the court had declared, was always unequal when it came to education.

Tomorrow, the old, unfair rules were to be changed. Elizabeth Eckford, in her own small way, would help change them.

A skilled young seamstress, Elizabeth put the finishing touches on a new outfit she had made to wear to school the next day. It was a pretty cotton dress, white with a black pattern dotting the lower part of the skirt. She wanted to look fresh and crisp on this first day of school. As she finished her sewing and ironing, Elizabeth had no suspicion that, after tomorrow, the homemade skirt would be seen by millions of people in newspaper photos across the United States and around the world.

Elizabeth, to her own great surprise, was about to become a very famous girl—and a very frightened one.

## Terror on the Way to School

The next day, Elizabeth dressed carefully and said prayers with her mother, who was a schoolteacher in another part of Little Rock. Elizabeth's mother was not happy about sending her daughter off to Central High School alone. Little Rock buzzed with rumors about the Ku Klux Klan and other racist groups trying to stop the African-American students from enrolling at Central High.

Threats had been uttered. Even stones had been thrown. A rock had smashed the window of a prominent African-American leader.[2] The Little Rock superintendent of schools had met with the African-American families to request that the entering students come alone, without their parents, to enroll. It would be safer, he assured the anxious families.

So on the morning of September 5, 1957, Elizabeth Eckford, carrying a new green notebook, took a public bus to a stop not far from Central High School. She had walked only a short distance from the bus stop when she realized that this would be no ordinary school day.

First, she heard a commotion—excited shouts and cries. Then, as she approached the school, she saw what a Little Rock newspaper would describe as "the incredible spectacle of a high school surrounded by National Guard troops."[3]

Orval Faubus, the forty-seven-year-old governor of Arkansas, had ordered the state guard to Central High supposedly to "maintain order" and "protect" the African-American students. Actually, the troops were there to keep the students out of the school. That morning, they had even turned away African-American janitors and workers in the school cafeteria.

Elizabeth now saw a solid line of uniformed men wearing steel helmets and armed with rifles. Standing shoulder to shoulder, they totally blocked the doors of Central High.

Elizabeth summoned the courage that would carry her through this terrible day. She approached the soldiers, looking for a way inside, but they lifted their rifles, blocking her entrance. When she realized there was no way through the armed line, and no sympathy in the grim white faces, Elizabeth was forced to turn back.

Where were the eight other African-American students who were supposed to start school at Central High today? Later, Elizabeth would learn that there had been a change of plans. The others were trying to enter as a group, although two became separated from

*Arkansas National Guardsmen direct Elizabeth Eckford away from Little Rock Central High on September 4, 1957.*

the rest. In the excitement and confusion of the morning, no one had told Elizabeth about the new arrangement. She found herself alone, facing the unyielding men in uniforms and a crowd of angry, shouting white people gathering near the entrance steps of the high school. Elizabeth saw Confederate flags, which she recognized as a symbol of racial hatred. Ku Klux Klan banners and signs were waved in angry defiance.

"Stop her!" someone was yelling. "Don't let her get away."

"Kill the nigger," another bystander screamed. "Kill her." (Such terrible racial slurs were common during the early years of the civil rights movement.) Shouts and catcalls rang on all sides as angry fists were shaken at Elizabeth. "Go back to Africa!"[4]

Elizabeth made her way toward the bus stop, moving steadily but never running. The mob closed in behind her, growing more menacing every moment. Elizabeth held her pace, not showing fear. She kept her silent dignity as slurs and insults rained around her. She turned toward a white woman who had a kindly expression. The woman spat in her face.

She tried to hold back her tears, tried to control her trembling as she approached the bench at the bus stop. Someone yelled, "Get a rope! Lynch her!"[5]

Elizabeth sat quietly on the bench, clasping her new school notebook. A white newspaper reporter from *The New York Times*, Benjamin Fine, sat beside the

*Elizabeth Eckford said she tried not to hear the racial slurs that members of the mob were yelling.*

terrified girl, putting his arm around her protectively. He tried to comfort her.

A woman pushed through the shouting mob, then turned back to face them. "Stop this! She's only a child!"[6] This woman, Grace Lorch, was one of the very few white members of the National Association for the Advancement of Colored People (NAACP) in Little Rock. She led Elizabeth, who was by now almost frozen with fear, toward a nearby drugstore where they could call a taxi.[7]

But the mob blocked the doors of the drugstore, shoving and pushing Elizabeth and her protector. Meanwhile, some of the crowd turned their hatred on

*Elizabeth Eckford sat on a bench waiting for a city bus after she was assailed by the Central High mob. Among the newsmen behind her was Dr. Benjamin Fine (wearing bow tie), the education reporter for* The New York Times.

reporter Benjamin Fine, spitting in his face and cursing him.

At last, a bus arrived. Elizabeth and Grace Lorch scrambled aboard, escaping the screams and threats of the crowd.

## All Are Turned Away

Meanwhile, one of Elizabeth's schoolmates, Melba Pattillo, was also driven away from Central High School by the mob. Other African-American students, however, reached the doors of the high school. There, they, too, were barred by soldiers and the howling protesters. At last, these six were delivered home in police cars.

Elizabeth's ordeal at the school and the bus stop had been recorded by news photographers that morning. The pictures were so remarkable that newspapers in many countries printed them. They showed the frightened girl sitting in quiet dignity, surrounded by jeering, hateful racists, their faces twisted in rage. Suddenly, the world knew what was happening at a school called Central High in a faraway city many people had never before heard of—Little Rock, Arkansas.

That hour at Central High would haunt Elizabeth Eckford long afterward. Nightmares would seize her and she would wake up screaming.[8] But for the time being, her first day at Central High was over.

The struggle at Little Rock's Central High was one of many battles in a long war against segregation. Segregation simply means separation, but the word has come to suggest being kept apart by force, usually for racial reasons: an involuntary separation imposed from outside.

# 2

# "SEPARATE IS UNEQUAL"

Segregation sprang from the racist belief of many whites in America that their own race was superior to other races. Racism went back to the days of slavery when African Americans were seen as property, not as humans. They were denied not only freedom, but the basic rights of life, such as education and physical protection. They could be bought and sold like cattle.

The gulf between slaves and free persons was made even wider by laws and social rules designed to keep the races apart. Whites and blacks were to have no contact except where African-American labor was needed. There could be no relationship between the races except as master and slave.

The Civil War (1861–1865) fought between the slaveholding South and the free North led to the

# $500 Reward

## FOR 13 NEGRO SLAVES.

The following described slaves were conveyed, by James De Baun and wife, by a regular deed of conveyance, executed on the 4th day of Sept., 1841, and duly recorded in the county of Pulaski, in this State, to Lambert Reardon, William E. Woodruff, and George C. Watkins, in trust, for the purpose of securing myself and others for certain liabilities, incurred as security for said De Baun; and, on the 22d day of April, 1843, said slaves were sold at public auction, by said trustees, at which sale I became the purchaser thereof, to wit: DANIEL, of dark complexion, aged 21 years; EVE, his wife, of light complexion, aged 26 years, and their two children, of light complexion—HARRIET, aged 10 years, and FELIX, aged 4 years; LITTLETON, a negro man, of dark complexion, aged 48 years; LUCY, his wife, of dark complexion, aged 28 years, and their three children—BETTY, a girl, of dark complexion, aged 5 years; FRANK, a boy, of dark complexion, aged 3 years, and ISRAEL, a child, of dark complexion, aged two years; EDMUND, of dark complexion, aged 21 years; EMELINE, his wife, of dark complexion, aged 18 years; HARRY, of dark complexion, aged 12 years; and CÆSAR, of dark complexion, aged 9 years.

The above reward of FIVE HUNDRED DOLLARS will be paid, by me, for the apprehension and delivery of said slaves, or in proportion for any part of them, to Gen. Wm. H. Overton, at Alexandria, Louisiana, or to James H. Leverech, Esq, in New-Orleans. Said negroes were removed from this county about two months since, at which time they were in charge of *Joseph Merril*, and are believed to be in his possession at this time, as the agent of said De Baun. He will probably endeavor to dispose of them, either in that capacity, or under a bill of sale from De Baun to him. Said slaves are believed to be in Texas, or on their way there; and all persons are forewarned from purchasing or harboring said slaves, under the severest penalties of the law, as they will be taken possession of, as my property, wherever they may be found.

ROSWELL BEEBE.

*Little Rock, Ark's, 24th April, 1843.*

This poster, printed in Little Rock in 1843, offers a reward for the return of slaves. It is now among the exhibits at the Central High Museum.

abolition of slavery and the adoption of new laws and constitutional amendments to guarantee civil rights to Americans regardless of race. For a few years during the post–Civil War era known as Reconstruction, the South was divided into districts. Each was commanded by a high-ranking military officer of the victorious Union Army. During this period, African Americans enjoyed some of the rights newly guaranteed to them by amendments to the United States Constitution. Black men, for instance, were allowed to vote, and some even held elective offices. Equal protection of the law for citizens of both races was widely enforced.[1]

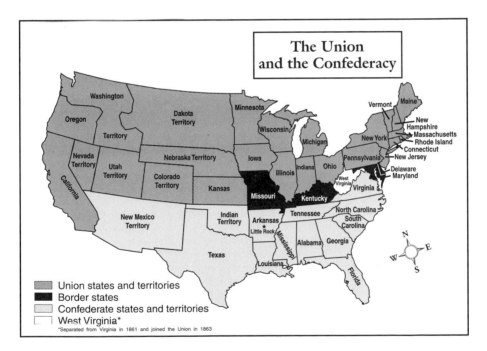

*Although Arkansas had been a slave state during the Civil War, Little Rock was generally known as a relatively harmonious town, where racial tensions were rare.*

But as soon as the Northern occupation troops left, local people took back control of their governments. For the most part, these leaders were former slave owners. Legally, they could not restore slavery. However, they were determined that African Americans should have only limited rights.[2] Leaders in the South seemed determined to re-create the world in which they had lived before the Civil War. Slavery could not exist, but they hoped to create social conditions as much like slavery as possible.

At first, there was some white resistance in the North to the oppressive new laws against African Americans in the South. The *Chicago Tribune* threatened that the Union armies would "convert the state of Mississippi into a frog pond" if the pro-segregation legislature of that state adopted the harsh, racist laws it was considering at the time.[3] That was in 1865, when the Civil War was fresh in the mind of the nation. Such reactions delayed some segregation laws a few years. But as time passed, many Americans stopped paying serious attention to what was happening in some faraway states. They had their own worries and interests to consider.

## Black Codes and Jim Crow

The former slaves suffered terribly from discrimination. Excuses were invented to deny them the right to vote, the right to education, and the right to equal treatment under the law. Regulations limiting and controlling the lives of African Americans were known as Black Codes. These Black Codes violated the United States Constitution and its promises of "equal protection under the law." But Southern courts, in particular, became skilled at twisting the meanings of words and blindly ignoring injustice.

Segregation, always at the heart of the Black Codes, was one weapon racists used to keep African Americans from exercising their newly won rights. Keeping the races apart at all times suggested that one group was superior to the other. This would "keep the Negroes in their place," as many Southern whites often said was their wish. This meant African Americans would be working at the hardest jobs for the lowest wages, attending the poorest schools, and living in the worst housing.[4] Segregation affected almost every area of life: transportation, sports, politics, jobs, churches, education, and even drinking fountains and lavatories.

Often segregation seemed just as hurtful in small matters as in large ones. Melba Pattillo, one of the young African-American students who tried to integrate Central High in Little Rock, Arkansas, recalled years later how she felt when she could not attend a performance by rock star Elvis Presley at Little Rock's segregated Robinson Auditorium: "As I sat in the middle of my bed among my stuffed animals looking at his picture in the ad, I was heartbroken that I couldn't go. . . . How many times had I asked my parents, 'Why? Why can't I go everywhere whites can go?'"[5]

Melba, like other African Americans, was a victim of rules called Jim Crow laws, named for a black character in variety show acts of the 1800s.[6] Jim Crow, played by whites who blackened their faces with burnt cork, grinned and shuffled foolishly to the delight of the racist audience. He was cowardly, lazy, and stupid. This, of course, was exactly what many whites wanted to believe about all blacks.

The Jim Crow laws, which served the same purpose as Black Codes, faced a challenge in court in 1896. Homer Plessy, an African American, was arrested in Louisiana when he sat in a railroad coach reserved for whites. Plessy felt that a law keeping him out of certain public railroad cars was a denial of the "equal protection" promised by the United States Constitution.[7]

A judge in New Orleans ruled that Plessy had no reason to complain, since there were "separate but equal" coaches on the train.[8] The United States Supreme Court agreed, and soon, almost all segregation laws were justified by the "separate but equal" policy. Despite claims to the contrary, the facilities and the schools reserved for blacks were uniformly inferior to those set aside for whites, often disgracefully so. In theory, whites were not allowed to use black-only facilities, so segregationists argued that the discrimination of Jim Crow laws went both ways. In reality, black-only facilities were so poor that no white person would voluntarily use them when superior facilities already existed for whites to use.

In countless places across the country, especially in rural districts, African-American children attended

## SOURCE DOCUMENT

IF THE TWO RACES ARE TO MEET UPON TERMS OF SOCIAL EQUALITY, IT MUST BE THE RESULT OF NATURAL AFFINITIES, A MUTUAL APPRECIATION OF EACH OTHER'S MERITS, AND A VOLUNTARY CONSENT OF INDIVIDUALS. [LEGISLATION] IS POWERLESS TO ERADICATE RACIAL INSTINCTS, OR TO ABOLISH DISTINCTIONS BASED UPON PHYSICAL DIFF-ERENCES, AND THE ATTEMPT TO DO SO CAN ONLY RESULT IN ACCENTUATING THE DIFFICULTIES OF THE PRESENT SITUATION. IF THE CIVIL AND POLITICAL RIGHTS OF BOTH RACES BE EQUAL, ONE CANNOT BE INFERIOR TO THE OTHER CIVILLY OR POLITICALLY. IF ONE RACE BE INFERIOR TO THE OTHER SOCIALLY, THE CONSTITUTION OF THE UNITED STATES CANNOT PUT THEM UPON THE SAME PLANE. . . .[9]

*In the controversial* Plessy v. Ferguson *ruling, the Supreme Court declared that segregation by race was legal so long as the facilities provided were "separate but equal."*

schools that were little more than shacks, freezing in cold weather, wet and leaky when it rained. Some cities spent four times as much to educate a white pupil as an African American. Even in Little Rock, which was considered one of the more progressive places in the South, students at black Dunbar High School studied from textbooks used first by white students at Central High, then handed down to black students. Unlike Central High, Dunbar had no gym, stadium, or prac- tice fields. It educated half as many students as Central but had only one third as many classrooms and a third as much space. The same inequality held true in teachers'

*Facilities were segregated throughout the South, keeping whites and blacks apart in everything from waiting rooms to drinking fountains.*

salaries and library books. Much of the money used to construct Dunbar came from private foundation grants, not tax money. The meager allotments to operate the school were public money. Central High, on the other hand, was well supported by tax dollars.[10] So Dunbar and Central, though certainly separate, were far from equal. Still, Dunbar was one of the better black public schools in the South. It was accredited by the North Central Association, a distinction among schools for African Americans.

## The African-American Awakening

For generations, African Americans had endured injustice more or less quietly. For the most part, they had little choice. Racist groups such as the Ku Klux Klan used violence and fear to keep African Americans from protesting their treatment. The Klan, founded in the Deep South after the Civil War, was a terrorist organization dedicated to preserving what its members saw as the traditional Southern way of life. Actually, this meant the use of violence and terrorism against African Americans and anyone else who did not share Klan views. The flaming cross—put on lawns to intimidate those who protested the unjust treatment of African Americans—was practically a Klan trademark. The cross supposedly symbolized the Christianity the Klan proclaimed, while the fire carried a threat of terrible violence. However, there was a new longing among blacks for change and serious talk about achieving it.

Famous artist Thomas Nast drew this depiction of how white supremacist organizations such as the Ku Klux Klan united with other racist groups to keep African Americans from exercising their newly won civil rights.

Meanwhile, countless African Americans, tired of racial injustice and poverty, were leaving the South to move to cities in Northern states. There, industrial jobs with better wages made the possibility of discrimination somewhat easier to bear. For most, it was a frightening step, leaving the only world they had ever known. But the hope of better lives beckoned them, and throngs traveled northward.[11]

When hundreds of thousands of African-American soldiers returned home after serving in World War II, public opinion began to shift. The black veterans had defended their country, sharing the risks with white soldiers. Now they wanted to share "at home the rights they had fought for overseas."[12] They were unwilling to live in a United States that tolerated lynching, segregation, and the violence used daily against African Americans.[13] Civil rights groups became active. Black communities awakened with new confidence and new determination.

This new demand for justice by blacks aroused white racists. Suddenly, lynchings, which had become rare, were back in the headlines. "Mobs assassinated no fewer than six Negro war veterans in a single three-week period" in the summer of 1946.[14]

In Monroe, Georgia, a mob of hooded men pulled an African-American war veteran, his wife, and another African-American couple out of a car, "lined the four of them up in front of a ditch, and . . . left a reported 180 bullet holes in one of the four corpses."[15]

Walter White, an African-American leader in the early struggle for civil rights, met with President Harry Truman in the Oval Office of the White House in 1946. He told Truman the shocking story of the Monroe lynchings. The president was astonished. "I had no idea it was as terrible as that," he exclaimed.[16]

Not long afterward, Truman became the first United States president to urge Congress to pass civil rights legislation, including a federal antilynching law.[17] Segregationists were so powerful politically, especially in the South, that even a law against racial murder was defeated in Congress. Such was the climate of violence when the struggle against school segregation began in the early 1950s.

## The Great Court Case

In 1953, seven-year-old Linda Brown was a pupil at a segregated school in Topeka, Kansas. Each morning, she had to walk two miles, then wait as much as half an hour for a bus to take her to her classroom. There was another school, a better one, very near her home, but it was for whites only.

Linda's father, the Reverend Oliver Brown, sued the Topeka Board of Education, demanding equal rights for his daughter. He demanded that Linda be able to go to the school nearest her home. Segregating the schools, Reverend Brown insisted, violated the equal treatment guaranteed by the United States Constitution.

At about the same time, five similar suits were filed by other African-American parents across the country. All these cases were grouped together in what is now known as *Brown* v. *Board of Education of Topeka, Kansas,* a landmark case in the struggle for racial equality. (It was called *Brown* because the families involved were listed alphabetically and the name Brown came first.)[18]

The National Association for the Advancement of Colored People (NAACP), a well-known civil rights organization, used its Legal Defense Fund to provide attorneys for the parents in the case. When the case reached the United States Supreme Court, it was argued by Thurgood Marshall, one of the greatest African-American civil rights attorneys of his time. (He later became the first African American appointed as a Supreme Court justice.)

Marshall knew about discrimination from personal experience. As a student, he was rejected by the law school of the University of Maryland because of his race. Instead, he attended Howard University's law school. Years later, he would argue before the Supreme Court the case that would force the Maryland law school to integrate.

As a young civil rights lawyer traveling through the South, Marshall often had to sleep and eat in his car because hotels and restaurants barred African Americans. He won twenty-nine of thirty-two cases he presented to the Supreme Court, but *Brown* in 1954 seemed to him the one that would most affect the future.

*The NAACP's chief counsel Thurgood Marshall (second from left) nudges through the crowd outside the Little Rock Federal District courtroom. Marshall argued the* Brown v. Board of Education *case before the Supreme Court in 1954. Later, he was appointed the first African-American justice of the United States Supreme Court.*

Marshall had reasons for both hope and fear as he worked on the *Brown* case. On one hand, the increase of violence in the South showed that racial hatred was powerful. Yet there were also signs that America was changing.

At this time, the United States was in fierce competition with the Communist Soviet Union to win the support of people and nations around the world. American racial prejudice and legal inequality gave powerful propaganda weapons to the Soviets. Why should the world believe that America was truly a democracy when its African-American citizens were treated unfairly and often brutally? Americans were starting to realize that it was important to show the world they were making progress in racial equality.

White civic and social organizations were also becoming interested in improving race relations. According to historian Richard Brisbane,

> Major groups, such as the American Friends Service Committee and the Anti-Defamation League of B'Nai B'rith [a Jewish organization], published reports and studies. . . . perhaps under directions from the Vatican, Roman Catholic prelates called for the elimination of discrimination and segregation from American life.[19]

Psychologist Kenneth Clark published studies showing that school segregation in itself had negative effects on African-American children: "A sense of in-born inferiority will follow many like an unwelcome shadow throughout their lives."[20]

This new awareness of the injustice long suffered by African Americans caused Walter White, executive director of the NAACP, to say, "American democracy is going forward."[21] Thurgood Marshall and other African-American leaders had high hopes when the great case of *Brown* v. *Board of Education of Topeka, Kansas* went before the Supreme Court.

The Court's justices also knew that a major turning point for the United States had arrived. Chief Justice Earl Warren, in particular, was eager to try to have all nine justices agree on the Court's decision in this historic matter.

## A Change for America

After hearing Marshall's case, the Supreme Court justices unanimously decided that the policy of "separate but equal" was simply a disguise for inequality. Chief Justice Earl Warren read the Court's ruling on May 17, 1954. Drawing on the findings of psychologist Kenneth Clark, Warren said:

> To separate [black children] from others of similar age and qualifications solely because of their race generates a feeling of inferiority. . . . [This] may affect their hearts and minds in a way unlikely ever to be undone. . . . We conclude that in the field of public education the doctrine of "separate but equal" has no place. Separate educational facilities are inherently unequal.[22]

This was one of the most important decisions the United States Supreme Court had ever made. The day after its announcement, President Dwight Eisenhower ordered the schools in the District of Columbia to be desegregated at once, to set an "example" for the rest of the nation.[23]

The *Voice of America* was the United States' radio information service broadcast to other countries. The *Voice* translated the Supreme Court's decision into thirty-four languages and broadcast the news around the

## SOURCE DOCUMENT

IN EACH OF [THESE] CASES, MINORS OF THE NEGRO RACE, THROUGH THEIR LEGAL REPRESENTATIVES, SEEK THE AID OF THE COURTS IN OBTAINING ADMISSION TO THE PUBLIC SCHOOLS OF THEIR COMMUNITY ON A NONSEGREGATED BASIS. IN EACH INSTANCE, THEY HAD BEEN DENIED ADMISSION TO SCHOOLS ATTENDED BY WHITE CHILDREN UNDER LAWS REQUIRING OR PERMITTING SEGREGATION ACCORDING TO RACE. . . .

TODAY, EDUCATION IS PERHAPS THE MOST IMPORTANT FUNCTION OF STATE AND LOCAL GOVERNMENTS. . . . [I]T IS DOUBTFUL THAT ANY CHILD MAY REASONABLY BE EXPECTED TO SUCCEED IN LIFE IF HE IS DENIED THE OPPORTUNITY OF AN EDUCATION. SUCH AN OPPORTUNITY, WHERE THE STATE HAS UNDERTAKEN TO PROVIDE IT, IS A RIGHT WHICH MUST BE MADE AVAILABLE TO ALL ON EQUAL TERMS. . . .

WE CONCLUDE IN THE FIELD OF PUBLIC EDUCATION THE DOCTRINE OF "SEPARATE BUT EQUAL" HAS NO PLACE. SEPARATE EDUCATIONAL FACILITIES ARE INHERENTLY UNEQUAL.[24]

*The Supreme Court, under the leadership of Chief Justice Earl Warren, ruled in 1954 that separate facilities, in regard to education, could not be equal, and that schools must be integrated.*

world to show that American democracy was marching forward.

For a hundred years, African Americans had been struggling against racism with only small results. Now an apparent miracle had occurred: "Black people wept and prayed and shouted hallelujah in innumerable Southern towns and cities."[25]

Lawyers for the NAACP and many other African-American leaders warned that a long, hard struggle lay ahead. The fight was just beginning.

## Segregationist Counterattack

Across the land, the segregationists prepared to do battle. In the Upper South, in such states as Tennessee and Arkansas, most people remained calm about the matter. But in the Deep South, known as the Black Belt, many governors, senators, mayors, and judges vowed to defy the Supreme Court to the point of shedding blood. There was even talk of taking up arms to continue where the Civil War had left off.[26]

A few whites in the South, a powerless minority, believed that school desegregation should start as soon as possible. A somewhat larger group, known as moderates, saw the Supreme Court as the highest authority in the nation. They did not like the idea of school integration, but would yield to the law. Integration, the moderates thought, could come gradually. That way, people would be upset as little as possible.

Only two weeks after the Supreme Court's decision, fourteen white men held a meeting in the town of Indianola, Mississippi. The questions before them were clear: How would they fight against integration in schools? How would they resist any other changes in Southern racial traditions?

At this meeting, the groups that would later be known as the White Citizens' Councils came into being. The councils swiftly spread across the South, preaching hatred and violence. Soon councils sprang up in most Southern cities.[27]

The councils and other segregationist groups banded together into an interstate organization called the Federation for Constitutional Government. This politically powerful association released a statement called the *Southern Manifesto*. One hundred one Southern members of Congress signed it, saying they would resist the Supreme Court's ruling and would even close down all the public schools of the South before accepting integration.

Meanwhile, the state of Arkansas remained quiet and cautious. Few people could have guessed that this was where the first crisis of school integration would soon take place with such violence that the nation could never forget it.

# 3

# 1956: A GATHERING STORM

The Deep South, which usually refers to South Carolina, Georgia, Florida, Alabama, Mississippi, and Louisiana, was once also known as the Cotton Belt. Cotton growing was once these states' main economic activity. The Deep South states held the majority of enslaved African Americans, who worked on the cotton, tobacco, and rice plantations. Not surprisingly, the Deep South was the very heart of the Confederacy (the Southern states that had left the Union) during the Civil War. In the years after the war, the strongest prejudice, worst violence, and most oppressive laws against African Americans could be found there.

To the north and west of the Deep South lie the border states, sometimes called the Upper South. Their traditions in racial matters are more varied, and usually less severe. Maryland and Kentucky are among these border states. All of the Southern states had strong segregation laws, but in response to the Supreme Court's *Brown* decision, border states— including Delaware, Kentucky, Missouri, Oklahoma, and part of Tennessee—quickly dropped racial barriers in schools.

In the Deep South, however, the segregationists raged against the *Brown* decision throughout 1956. It did not soothe them to know that schools in Northern states had been integrated for years. They watched neighboring Southern border states end segregation and felt besieged. The Deep South searched for ways to strike back.

"Impeach Earl Warren!" became a common yell at segregationist rallies. Southern state legislatures passed laws to avoid the Court's order.[1] Some places closed the public schools. In Virginia, school closings locked out twelve thousand pupils of both races.[2] A segregationist group in Florida printed posters demanding "Death to all Race Mixers! Keep White Public Schools White. . . . Shoot the Race-Mixing Invaders!"[3]

## Little Rock Plans Integration

In the midst of this uproar, the state of Arkansas remained calm. It already had some good examples to follow. The University of Arkansas had integrated its law school long before the Supreme Court's decision in *Brown*. The university's graduate center in Little Rock had also admitted blacks, as did its medical school. Two public school districts had been integrated with no trouble.

Little Rock, the state capital, was a city of one hundred twenty thousand people in 1955. About a quarter of these were African Americans. Founded on the banks of the sweeping Arkansas River in the center of the state, Little Rock was proud of its clean, safe streets and gracious neighborhoods. The city enjoyed a reputation as a progressive, civilized community.

Visitors from other Southern towns were startled to see some African Americans as members of the police force. Blacks served on juries, rode on integrated buses, and used the integrated city library with no fuss. One third of eligible African Americans were registered voters, a remarkably high number for a Southern city in the 1950s.[4] In spite of these encouraging signs, however, there existed some painful examples of segregation: Many schools, restaurants, theaters, and waiting rooms were restricted by race.

The racial scene had not always been so calm and progressive. Back in 1927, Little Rock Nine student Elizabeth Eckford's mother had witnessed a Little Rock lynching when an African-American man was murdered and burned.[5] In spite of such memories, Little Rock appeared to be a city that might become a model of peaceful public school integration. While school boards and authorities in other places fumed, protested, and balked, Little Rock began planning an orderly desegregation of its schools.

Only five days after *Brown* was announced in 1954, the Little Rock school board declared that it would comply with the new policy. At the same time, the board members complained that the Court had provided no clear guidelines on how to desegregate. This lack of clarity caused problems and confusion in many

*A statue named "Opportunity" stands near the entrance to Central High. But African-American students, walking past the building to reach their own segregated schools, knew that the educational opportunities of Central High School were not open to them.*

places. But Little Rock went ahead with its planning, assigning the job to superintendent of schools Virgil Blossom. That summer of 1954, while all the schools were closed for vacation, Blossom developed his plan.

The city was then building two new high schools, which were scheduled to open in 1956. These, Blossom suggested, would be integrated. Junior high schools and elementary schools were to be desegregated later.

Planning for a slow relaxing of the racial barriers was still in progress when the Supreme Court, realizing the vagueness of its first decision, ruled again. How and when must the schools desegregate? "With all deliberate speed," said the Supreme Court, in a decision often referred to as *Brown II*. Still, no exact deadline for school integration was set.

The second ruling caused the Little Rock school board to make and adopt a new version of Blossom's plan. Only one new high school would be integrated and with only a limited number of students in the upper three grades.

Black families reacted unfavorably. They recognized a tactic of stalling. They rejected Blossom's explanation that a "rush" to desegregate would be too upsetting for the city. One member of the school board had said frankly that the new plan was "developed to provide as little integration as possible for as long as possible legally."[6]

## The Segregationists Rally

In the next few months, a harsher face of Arkansas emerged. For the most part, residents of the city of Little Rock had always been better educated and more open to change than people in some other parts of the state. The more isolated and often poorer areas had long resented city ways and ideas. They distrusted the state capital, considering it snobbish and lacking traditional values. Now rural communities began to make their angry voices heard.

Enemies of integration arrived from remote farms and villages of Arkansas to protest. Enraged racists even came from other states to voice their opinions.[7]

They demanded to know how "race mixing" could be prevented at school dances. What about sharing lavatories? The segregationists played on every old fear and prejudice of the crowds they attracted. They predicted that African Americans would soon be "taking over everything." Interracial marriages would soon become common. White jobs would be lost to cheaper black labor.

At about the same time, other events alarmed many white people. In Montgomery, Alabama, Reverend Dr. Martin Luther King, Jr., "led a silent, maddeningly nonviolent black army" in a successful struggle for equality on city buses.[8]

African Americans won another civil rights battle when the huge public school system of Louisville, Kentucky, dropped all racial barriers without trouble

*Dr. Martin Luther King, Jr., was one of the foremost civil rights activists at the time of the Little Rock crisis.*

or resistance.[9] These African-American victories stood as serious threats to white racists.

But some events encouraged the segregationists. In Mansfield, Texas, African-American pupils tried to enroll in a public school and were met by a band of thugs who intended to beat them. Texas Governor Allan Shivers ordered the Texas Rangers, a state police force, not to uphold the Supreme Court's decision, but instead to force the children back to an all-black school.

In Little Rock, the NAACP went back to court to demand that all grades be integrated at once. The civil

*Rallying against school desegregation, this student motorcade paused in front of the Arkansas State Capitol.*

rights organization won only a partial victory, but the main result was that Central High School was ordered to admit African-American students without further delay. Time had run out for the reluctant school board.

## Nine Students Are Chosen

In the spring of 1957, Little Rock teachers in black-only Dunbar High School and the new Horace Mann High School made a list of students who would like to transfer to Central High the next September. This led to a cautious selection process by the school board. Students who had poor disciplinary records were dropped from consideration. Having good grades was important, too.

Parents were warned that their children might have problems changing to a new school that had never before admitted African Americans. Of seventy-five students who had first asked to transfer, the final list was whittled down to ten. Then one student dropped out, so the final list had nine names. These students would be known to history as the Little Rock Nine.

Only one of them was a senior: Ernest Green had an outstanding record as a Boy Scout Eagle Badge winner and a member of the National Honor Society. Six of the students were going to enter Central High as juniors: Minnijean Brown, Elizabeth Eckford, Thelma Mothershed, Melba Pattillo, Gloria Ray, and Terrence Roberts. Jefferson Thomas and Carlotta Walls would enroll in Central High as sophomores.

Late in the summer, superintendent of schools Virgil Blossom called a meeting for the nine students and their parents. A dreary picture of their future at Central High was revealed: They would not be allowed to participate in team sports. There would be no participation in social or service clubs for them, no school dances, and no playing in either of the school's two bands. "This is because you are transfer students," they were told.[10] But the nine students all knew this was a thin excuse. They were being restricted because of race. The prospect was saddening.

For Carlotta Walls, the restrictions meant giving up her activities in the National Honor Society and in the student council. Ernest Green would be barred from the Central High bands, even though he was a talented tenor saxophone player who played outside of school with an amateur group called the Jazzmen. Jefferson Thomas had the proven ability to become a track star, but when he went to Central High, he would not be given the chance.

If the idea of this meeting was to convince some of the students to change their minds about entering Central High, then the plan failed. Central High meant new opportunities, a better education. The Little Rock Nine would not be discouraged.

So, as the summer of 1957 drew to a close, these nine students waited and wondered what the future would bring.

# THE SURROUNDED HIGH SCHOOL

Many people served bravely in the struggle to integrate Central High School, but none was more important than Daisy Bates, leader of the Arkansas NAACP.

Daisy Bates knew about racial violence firsthand. When she was only a baby, her mother had been murdered by white racists. Daisy herself had grown up in the shadow of threats and hatred. With her husband, L. C. Bates, she was active as a newspaper publisher. She was thus a target of racial terrorism. Most white residents of Little Rock simply disagreed with the Bateses' politics and civil rights activities. But many members of the White Citizens' Council and the Ku Klux Klan truly hated L. C. and Daisy Bates. They saw the Bateses as dangerous rebels who were trying to destroy society.

Before the start of the school year at Central High, Daisy Bates met with the nine African-American students. "Ignore racial slurs and avoid confrontations," she urged.[1] Bates knew that the eyes of the world

*L. C. Bates, husband of Arkansas NAACP chapter president Daisy Bates, carved the turkey at a Thanksgiving dinner with the Little Rock Nine in November 1957.*

would be on this group, and she did everything possible to build up their confidence.

During the summer of 1957, she watched the rising tension in Little Rock. She feared that the city was going "to become a battle ground."[2]

Groups organized to promote racial prejudice sprang up. One segregationist society called itself the Mothers League of Central High School. Daisy Bates quickly found out, however, that very few of its members actually had children attending Central High. Meanwhile, the newly formed Capital Citizens' Council was also working all summer to pressure Arkansas Governor Orval Faubus to resist the Supreme Court's integration decision.

In late August, the Citizens' Council hosted a dinner for three hundred segregationists. Governor Marvin Griffin of Georgia was one speaker who was present. "People of Arkansas," he shouted, "join my people of Georgia in determined resistance to the crime of integration!" The crowd clapped and cheered as Governor Griffin predicted the end of American democracy, "if the South surrenders her schools to the operation of the federal government."[3] The aroused listeners stamped their feet, whistled in approval, and the hall resounded with rebel yells.

The Georgia governor succeeded in stirring up violence. Later that night, a rock was hurled through Daisy Bates's window. The message wrapped around it said, "Stone this time. Dynamite next." As she looked at the shattered glass on her living room rug, Daisy

Bates said to her husband, "We are at war in Little Rock."[4]

## Governor Faubus

As the battle lines were being drawn, Governor Orval Faubus remained a puzzling figure. Faubus was born and raised in a corner of the state where almost no African Americans had ever lived. Indeed, he was a grown man before he ever saw a black person. His own father was a Socialist, a political persuasion unusual in the United States and almost unheard of in rural Arkansas. The senior Faubus believed in public ownership of industry, wide programs of social welfare, and a large measure of racial equality. He seemed to be a radical to his back-country neighbors. Early in life, Orval appeared to share his father's views. Later, he became more traditional and denied or shrugged off his youthful opinions. Governor Faubus, throughout his political career, had been thought of as moderate in racial matters. No one could be sure what he would do now in the Little Rock crisis.

Governor Faubus would soon have to stand for re-election, and he knew his rivals would be die-hard segregationists. Certainly, the governor would look to his political future when he decided what course to take. Meanwhile, he delayed taking action by talking about possible ways to avoid the *Brown* decision. All the governor's possible plans were clearly unconstitutional, a smoke screen to give Faubus more time to

Over the years, Governor Orval Faubus made the Arkansas state legislature a reflection of his own opinions. This cartoon shows a session where all the office holders are clones, or copies, of the governor. Even the paintings and sculptures are Faubuses.

decide before committing himself to any course of action.

On August 27, as the first day of school approached, the Mothers League went to court to halt the planned desegregation of Central High. They could do this by obtaining a written order, called an injunction, against the school board's plan to integrate.

No surprises were expected in the courtroom. Then, Governor Orval Faubus himself suddenly appeared as a witness at the public hearing. Faubus reported dramatic news, truly startling developments. Black and white teenagers, he said, were buying knives and guns at an alarming rate. He felt that riots and bloodshed could be expected at the opening of Central High.

No one else had heard of this rush to gun shops. In fact, later investigations failed to find any increase in the sale of deadly weapons in the Little Rock area. But the governor's words were instantly accepted as truth by the many people who wanted to prevent the Little Rock Nine from entering Central High. The Mothers League injunction was granted by the judge because of the governor's prediction of violence. The nine students would not be admitted to Central High until further court action was taken.

## The Flaming Cross

Daisy Bates never forgot the fearful night that followed. With loud honking of horns, the city's racists drove

*Arkansas Governor Orval Faubus (left) and Little Rock school superintendent Virgil Blossom at a 1958 press conference.*

past her house, yelling threats and curses. "The coons won't be going to Central!" they shouted.[5]

Already, the NAACP had filed a petition to end the injunction, pointing out that it was based on exaggerated threats and frightening falsehoods about weapons. Governor Faubus, at almost the same time, was challenged to give his information about gun sales to the Federal Bureau of Investigation (FBI) to be evaluated. He evaded the request, saying that his sources were "too vague."[6] A federal judge ordered integration at Central High to go ahead without further interference.

The threats became even more menacing. One night, a fiery cross eight feet tall was set aflame on the

Bateses' lawn. A crude message was left: "Go back to Africa! KKK."[7] The Ku Klux Klan (KKK) had often used flaming crosses to frighten blacks, Jews, Catholics, and immigrants.

While the Klan used threats to dishearten the integrationists, Governor Faubus was quietly and secretly plotting his own ambush against integration. Faubus had carefully calculated the fears and prejudices of the voters of Arkansas. He had decided that, if he could turn back the African Americans, keeping Central High all-white, he would be politically invincible in the state. His re-election, perhaps even his endless re-election, seemed assured. Arkansas had no term limits, a huge majority of whites opposed integration, and there were not enough African-American voters to make a real difference. Carefully, Governor Faubus laid his plans.[8]

## The Faubus Bombshell

The governor launched his surprise attack on Labor Day, September 2, 1957. Daisy Bates learned of it in the evening when a reporter came to her house. "Mrs. Bates, do you know that national guardsmen are surrounding Central High?" he asked.[9]

Daisy Bates and her husband, L. C., hurried to the school. There, several hundred soldiers dressed for battle were climbing out of army trucks.

At almost the same time, 10:15 P.M. on Monday, Faubus went on television to make a speech. He began harmlessly, outlining Arkansas' progressive record in

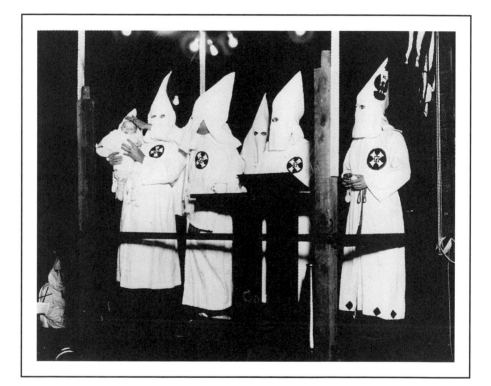

*Because racist groups such as the Ku Klux Klan had used violence in the past to keep African Americans from exercising their rights, the parents of the Little Rock Nine feared for their children's safety as they tried to integrate Central High School.*

race relations and explaining his own part in this advancement: Public buses, a few schools, and political parties had been integrated. African Americans had been hired in state government jobs.

Then he came to his point: There was a looming danger of violence and disorder at Central High. The police had informed him of the sale of large numbers of weapons in Little Rock. Black youths, he said, were buying knives at one store and guns at others. Even as Faubus spoke, a statewide telephone network was working to assemble a huge crowd of probably violent protesters at Central High at 6:00 A.M. on Tuesday. Then Faubus told the shocked viewers:

> I have reports of caravans that will converge upon Little Rock from many points of the state. . . . Some of these groups have already reached the city—are here now—and some of the information of these caravans has come to me from the school authorities themselves. . . . Blood will run in the streets. . . .[10]

According to historian Roy Reed, Faubus said that "'Because of the harm that may occur on the morrow,' [t]he troops would not act as segregationists or integrationists. But order and peace could not be maintained if forcible integration went ahead."[11]

The governor's speech electrified Little Rock. Thousands of telephones rang across the city as alarmed people sought news. Had anyone seen the caravans? Was there gunfire? Were buildings burning?

The next hours were frantic for everyone involved in the Central High integration crisis. School officials gathered in an emergency meeting and decreed that the African-American students should not try to enroll at Central High.

The parents of the Little Rock Nine, alarmed about their children's safety, simply did not know what to do. Daisy Bates, already realizing that Governor Faubus was being less than truthful, went ahead with her plans. The NAACP returned to the United States district court. There, the judge ordered the Central High integration to go ahead at once.

The families of the Little Rock Nine and superintendent Virgil Blossom met hastily. The students would come to Central High in the morning without their parents. The presence of African-American adults might arouse violence, Blossom said.[12]

Also concerned about violence, Daisy Bates requested a police escort for the nine students. Then, she began calling the nine families, asking them to meet her several blocks from Central High. The police would drive them the rest of the distance to the high school.

Everyone agreed to Daisy Bates's plan except the Eckfords. They had no telephone, so Bates reminded herself to pass by their house in the morning.

Then, as she later said, "Tired in mind and body, I decided to handle the matter early in the morning."[13] So the Eckfords did not know about the change of plans. Elizabeth would be on her own.

# THE SCREAMING EAGLES ARE SUMMONED

*Maybe going to Central High isn't such a good idea after all. It is costing my family a lot of agony and energy, and I haven't even attended one day yet. Will Grandma always have to sit up guarding us?*

—Diary of Little Rock Nine student Melba Pattillo[1]

Early the next morning, Daisy Bates learned what was happening to Elizabeth Eckford on her car radio. There was nothing she could do to rescue Elizabeth. Her own situation was serious enough as she and seven of the African-American students, escorted by the police, drew near to Central High.

At the same time, Melba Pattillo was on foot not far from Central High with her mother. They were on their way to meet Daisy Bates and the others. Melba saw a "strange parade" of white people, such a big crowd that there was no room on the sidewalks. They walked on grass and in the street, pushing and jostling. Melba saw a mob of angry men and women shaking their fists and shouting, "Niggers, go home! Niggers, go back where you belong."[2] Others were repeating a chant, almost dancing, "Two, four, six, eight, we ain't gonna integrate!"[3]

Her mother pulled her by the arm, searching for the rest of the African-American group, hoping for safety in numbers. At a distance, they heard the mob shouting at Elizabeth Eckford, "Get her, get the nigger out of there. Hang her . . . !"[4]

A white man seized Melba Pattillo, yelling, but she struggled free. She and her mother ran from another

*Saying that he was acting under orders from Governor Faubus, Lieutenant Colonel Marion Johnson of the Arkansas National Guard used his nightstick to block the path of Carlotta Walls and Jefferson Thomas as they tried to enter Central High School.*

man who was carrying a rope. Mrs. Pattillo's blouse was ripped, and she had to abandon her high-heeled shoes so she could run faster. They reached their car and took shelter as one man pounded on the hood and another hurled a brick at the windshield.

At last, they reached the protection of the police and the other students. But Daisy Bates's group had no success in getting through the line of National Guardsmen. The soldiers were under orders to keep the African-American students out of the school and would not listen to any arguments or pleas.

## Calling on the President

The African-American students were at last delivered back to their homes. Daisy Bates, with other NAACP officials, went to see the federal district court judge. The judge lost no time in asking President Dwight D. Eisenhower to order a government probe of Governor Faubus's armed resistance.

There was some uncertainty about how the president would respond. His record on civil rights was mixed: He had supported integration in the District of Columbia and had continued President Harry Truman's integration of the United States armed forces. Yet he was clearly reluctant to push civil rights legislation forward with any vigor. Now, however, he saw a clear matter of upholding the law. Eisenhower responded at once. "I took an oath to support and defend the Constitution," he told Governor Faubus in a telegram.[5] Eisenhower meant that the Supreme

Court had made a ruling, and as president, it was his duty to enforce it.

Faubus refused to cooperate by removing his National Guard troopers. The two sides had reached a standstill. The governor of Arkansas was now standing in outright defiance of the federal government.

Central High seemed quiet for the next few days, while the armed Arkansas National Guard stayed on duty there. Daisy Bates obtained assignments of school work from Central High teachers, so the Little Rock Nine could work at her house and not fall behind in their classes. They continued living at their own homes but she supervised their studies.

Meanwhile, the world was reacting to the situation in Little Rock. Photographs of Elizabeth Eckford, a helpless young girl menaced by an ugly mob, appeared on front pages of newspapers in world capitals, including Rome and Moscow.

The mayor of Little Rock, Woodrow Mann, reacting to the terrible international publicity, condemned the governor: "Faubus has caused trouble where there wasn't any!"[6] As a result of these words, Mayor Mann found a cross burning in his yard in the early morning of September 6. This threat, however, did not silence him. He repeated that Faubus had invented the story about possible violence, and now he claimed that violence was being manufactured "to keep the citizens keyed up."[7]

But many racists in Little Rock and across the country hailed Faubus as a hero. At the end of a week

*Although President Dwight D. Eisenhower did not firmly support the concept of integration, as a soldier he believed commands had to be followed and he was prepared to enforce the ruling of the Supreme Court.*

of deadlock, an army helicopter landed on the lawn of Eisenhower's vacation home in Rhode Island. It carried Governor Faubus. He was to meet with the president.

Faubus and Eisenhower talked privately for twenty minutes. Dwight "Ike" Eisenhower had spent his life as a soldier; maintaining order was important to him. He had sympathy with local and state traditions, but there was no doubt that he would enforce the law. No one knows exactly what was said in his talk with the Arkansas governor, but Eisenhower clearly thought Faubus had surrendered. The troops would be promptly removed from Central High, Eisenhower announced. Herbert Brownell, the United States attorney general and a supporter of civil rights, however, suspected that Faubus was stalling. Brownell's suspicion proved to be right.

## Faubus Plays a Delaying Game

For a week, National Guard soldiers remained outside Central High while Faubus defended his position, predicting a mass of protesters "armed to the teeth with repeating rifles."[8] The FBI looked into the governor's claims and found that they were based on nothing but rumors. Faubus was ordered by the federal district court to remove the National Guard.

Finally, on Monday, September 22, the Little Rock Nine, after saying prayers, started for Central High. The state troopers were gone, but a mob of more than a thousand protesters had assembled to block the doors of the school. The Little Rock police, on hand to protect the African-American students, did not recognize members of the crowd except for a few "well-known troublemakers."[9] The others were strangers, probably people from other towns. Assistant police chief Eugene Smith wondered if the governor's aides had encouraged these protesters to converge on Little Rock.[10]

"Here they come!" someone yelled. The crowd surged forward. They had mistaken four black reporters for parents of the Little Rock Nine. Bricks and bottles sailed through the air. Reporter Alex Wilson, on assignment for the *New Amsterdam News,* bent in pain, trying to shield himself as a racist kicked him repeatedly in the stomach.

The black reporters had distracted the mob, and the nine students slipped into a side door of Central

*Reporter Alex Wilson was beaten by the mob as the Little Rock Nine entered Central High School on September 23, 1957.*

High. A woman screamed, "My daughter's in there with those niggers. Oh, my God!"[11]

The crowd charged the police barricades, smashing them. They turned their fury on several white journalists from *Life* magazine, knocking them down, destroying cameras and recorders.

Inside, the nine students waited uncertainly in a hall. They could still hear the bedlam outside, but Central High was, for the moment, integrated.

In the classrooms, things were not as bad as the African-American students had expected. A few white students marched out when blacks joined the classes, but some others were at least encouraging if not friendly. "It's the grown-ups, not the kids, causing all the trouble," one white girl said.[12]

At noon, the situation outside was almost beyond control. The Little Rock Nine were spirited out a delivery entrance into police cars while the mob raged and howled at the school doors.

The city of Little Rock became a battlefield that night. Windows were smashed, bottles and bricks broke street lights, rocks thudded on porches. Several black drivers were reportedly dragged from their cars and beaten.[13]

The Bates home was guarded by armed officers, and L. C. Bates kept a pistol handy. When a car that had been slowly circling the Bates house was halted, police discovered a bundle of dynamite.

The Little Rock Nine, Daisy Bates decided, could not again risk their lives at Central High until their

*African-American students were hurried out of a side door at Central High by police escorts on the first day of the school's integration.*

---

**SOURCE DOCUMENT**

IT WAS EXACTLY LIKE AN EXPLOSION, A HUMAN EXPLOSION.

AT 8:35 A.M., THE PEOPLE STANDING IN FRONT OF THE HIGH SCHOOL LOOKED LIKE THE ONES YOU SEE EVERY DAY IN A SHOPPING CENTER. . . . ORDINARY PEOPLE—MOSTLY CURIOUS, YOU WOULD HAVE SAID—WATCHING A HIGH SCHOOL ON A BRIGHT, BLUE-AND-GOLD MORNING.

FIVE MINUTES LATER, AT 8:40, THEY WERE A MOB.

THE TERRIFYING SPECTACLE OF 200-ODD INDIVIDUALS, SUDDENLY WELDED TOGETHER INTO A SINGLE BODY, TOOK PLACE IN THE BAREST FRACTION OF A SECOND. IT WAS AN EXPLOSION, SAVAGERY CHAIN-REACTING FROM PERSON TO PERSON, FUSING THEM INTO A WHITE-HOT MASS. . . .

A STRANGE, ANIMAL GROWL ROSE FROM THE CROWD. "HERE COME THE NEGROES."[14]

---

*Relman Mori, who won a Pulitzer Prize for covering the Little Rock crisis, wrote this account of the first day of school in 1957.*

safety was guaranteed. But who could guarantee it? "The President of the United States," said Daisy Bates.[15]

## A Forced Showdown

It soon became clear that the president had little choice. It was generally believed that Eisenhower disagreed with the *Brown* v. *Board of Education* decision. Some people believed that he had tried to persuade Chief Justice Earl Warren to vote against integration.

But now Eisenhower received telegrams from Little Rock's congressman and from Mayor Woodrow Mann. Send help, the telegrams said. Mayor Mann's telegram was sent in defiance of the blazing cross that had been burned in his yard.

President Eisenhower issued a historic order: Armed United States troops would be dispatched to Little Rock. In addition, the Arkansas National Guard of ten thousand soldiers would no longer be under Governor Faubus's control. These troops could not again be used to obstruct the law.

Within minutes, one thousand paratroopers at Fort Campbell, Kentucky, were ordered to Little Rock. Within hours, they were on the way to Arkansas in eight giant transport planes.[16] The troops selected for the Little Rock mission were part of the crack 101st Airborne Division of the 327th Infantry Regiment, nicknamed the Screaming Eagles.

It was growing dark in Little Rock when residents heard the drone of aircraft bound for the nearby air base. Soon afterward, a police escort with wailing sirens and flashing lights guided a long line of army vehicles through the astonished city to Central High. No American city had witnessed such a scene since the Civil War.

Citizens poured from houses near Central High to stand watching on porches and in yards. They saw gas masks, rifles, bayonets, and clubs being unloaded. One thing they did not see was a black soldier, although there were many African-American members of the 101st Airborne. Most of those soldiers had remained in the Little Rock armory as reserves. The army did not want the racist mob to see black soldiers at Central High and use this as an excuse for rioting.

On lawns near the Central High tennis courts, army pup tents and field kitchens suddenly sprouted. Shade trees served as posts to hold communication wires. All approaches to the school were heavily guarded. Central High was firmly in the hands of the Screaming Eagles.

# STUDENT PERSECUTION

$O$n the first day of integration enforced by the army at Central High, General Edwin Walker, commander of the Screaming Eagles, spoke to the white students. "You have nothing to fear from my soldiers," he told them. "However . . . I intend to use all means necessary to prevent any interference with . . . your school board's plan."[1]

Meanwhile, a block from the school, Major James Meyer and a small group of soldiers faced a mob. The racists, shouting threats and insults, refused to obey the major's order to disperse. They defied him until thirty more soldiers, summoned by radio, arrived wearing steel helmets and carrying rifles with bayonets fixed.

The soldiers moved slowly but assuredly into the crowd, which gave way before them. The street lay quiet. Another skirmish in the battle of Little Rock was over.

## The Little Rock Nine Make History

A few minutes later, the nine African-American students, looking serious and determined, marched into

*General Edwin Walker, in charge of the Screaming Eagles who were sent to enforce the integration order, walks in front of Central High.*

Central High School. An army helicopter circled above them while three hundred fifty paratroopers stood at attention.[2]

Immediately, the black students were confronted by hostility from the school administration. They were all assigned to different classes and different home-rooms, so they could not draw support from each other. "Why?" one of the students asked.

The answer came from an unidentified male teacher with an angry, booming voice: "You wanted integration . . . you got integration!"[3]

*United States 101st Airborne troops helped Carlotta Walls (left) and Minnijean Brown (right) from a government station wagon when they arrived to begin classes on September 25, 1957.*

When Melba Pattillo took her seat in class, the other students promptly moved away from her. A boy shouted at the teacher, "Are you gonna let that nigger coon sit in our class?" The teacher ignored the question. The boy then told the other students, "We can kick the crap out of this nigger. . . . They ain't nothing but animals."[4]

After the first day at Central High, there was a meeting of the Little Rock Nine at the home of Daisy Bates. Bates had mixed feelings about the "victory." She said that when it took an army "to assure nine

Negro children their constitutional right in a democratic society, I can't be happy."[5]

Ernest Green, the sole senior among the black students, also felt the day's triumph was lessened because it was forced at gunpoint. But he added, "I don't intend to quit."[6]

That same day, a white student named Robin Woods remarked to a newspaper reporter, "That was the first time I'd ever gone to school with a Negro, and it didn't hurt a bit."[7]

Another student was less easy-going about the situation. Senior-class member Coy Vance told the *Arkansas Gazette*, "If they don't have guards with them niggers, they're going to be murdered."[8] An anonymous sixteen-year-old white female student offered a solution to the problem: "If parents would just go home and let us alone, we'd be all right. . . . We just want them to leave us be. We can do it."[9]

## Reaction to Integration

Governor Faubus, however, had not surrendered. In the midst of the fear and uncertainty that gripped Little Rock, he delivered a speech that seemed deliberately designed to cause more trouble and to gain further political credit for himself with those who disagreed with integration.

After claiming on television that the Arkansas capital was now "occupied territory," Faubus went on to charge that the federal soldiers were "bludgeoning innocent bystanders." He insisted that "the warm red blood of an American city" was being "spilled in the streets."[10]

It was possible that Faubus had truly believed in the dangers he had warned against when he called out the National Guard. But now he had shown his true colors. His television speech about the behavior of the United States Army in Little Rock was simply made up of lies. Faubus could see the real situation. However, he deliberately tried to scare people by exaggerating. Later, he alarmed parents by saying that soldiers were entering "girls' lavatories" at Central High.[11] No support for this charge was ever found.

Over the next weeks, the segregationists changed their tactics. Discovering that they could not succeed outside the school, they tried to attack on the inside. Some of those who had sons and daughters attending Central High used their children as weapons against the Little Rock Nine.

White students hurled rocks and eggs at the black students in October. Unidentified vandals broke into lockers to destroy property. Ink was thrown at the African Americans so often that they all began to keep extra clothes at school. A bottle bomb was planted in a locker, and fake bomb scares interrupted studies time after time.

Jefferson Thomas suffered the worst physical attack, when he was knocked unconscious from behind. Carlotta Walls carried her books as a shield against sudden punches. Melba Pattillo fled from an outdoor sports field when a group of women claiming to be "mothers of Central High students" assailed her during a physical education class. African-American students suffered kicks and shoving. All of them at times went home bruised and bloody.[12]

## Minnijean Defends Herself

Minnijean Brown could not keep herself from fighting back. She felt there was no humiliation she had not endured, after having been kicked, spat on, shouted at, and assaulted. She tried to follow the nonviolent teachings then being taught widely by civil rights leader Reverend Dr. Martin Luther King, Jr. Daisy Bates had also counseled the Little Rock Nine to ignore abuse, even to reply "Thank you" when it was at all possible. But sometimes the torments were too provoking for Minnijean to stand.

This was the case one day at lunch hour when two white boys jostled her and blocked her way in the cafeteria line. A bowl of chili sat on a lunch tray. Minnijean dumped it over one of her surprised attackers. The African-American cafeteria employees, who had always been silent before, burst into a round of applause for the plucky girl.[13]

Minnijean suffered a brief school suspension for her behavior, but even then her troubles were not over. After putting up with a long series of slurs and humiliations, Minnijean turned on an abusive white girl and returned a racist slur in kind. She later said, "I turned and screamed, 'White trash! Why don't you leave me alone?'"[14] Later, Minnijean explained that she really had not known just how insulting the words would be. But the incident, combined with her history of resistance, led to her expulsion from Central High.

Minnijean's high school career was not over, however. The excellent New Lincoln School in New York City offered Minnijean a scholarship. A college professor and his wife made her welcome at their home there.

To celebrate Minnijean's removal from Central High, small cards were passed among students. They read: "One down, eight to go." The same words were on signs worn by two white students who were suspended for "disruptive conduct." That same day, a white boy was expelled for pushing Gloria Ray of the Little Rock Nine down a flight of stairs.

## The Struggle Worsens

The Mothers League of Central High organized an event that was anything but motherly. It arranged for some white students to march dramatically out of the high school, then lynch and burn a straw-stuffed dummy of a black student. Meanwhile, the youthful racists yelled, cheered, and danced. Nearby paratroopers put an end to the ugly display.[15]

Many Little Rock citizens were outraged when photos of the burning appeared in newspapers across the country, again disgracing the Arkansas capital. It had begun to dawn on some residents that such publicity might drive away business and cost them money.[16]

The persecution of the Little Rock Nine remained so intense and so prolonged that it has been mistakenly thought that most white students at Central High played a part in it. Actually, the troublemakers numbered only about seventy-five out of more than two thousand teenagers enrolled.[17] Still, the great majority of white students silently supported the segregationists.

The active troublemakers made up in noise what they lacked in numbers as they screamed threats in the school's halls and stairways. Some white students who befriended or had merely been civil to the African Americans were also attacked. They were greeted with raucous shouts of "Nigger lover!" The treatment of their supporters added a burden of guilt to the Little Rock Nine, even though such behavior was clearly not their fault.

Teachers at Central High seemed divided. Most of them stood firmly against integration. They would not make an effort to help it succeed. Ernest Green's physics teacher refused to let him make up work missed during the first violent weeks of the semester. Physics, Ernest was told, was too difficult a subject "for a Negro."[18] Ernest hired a tutor and met the challenge. Several other teachers, however, whatever their private feelings were, treated the African Americans with careful fairness. Later, one segregationist Little Rock school board member claimed that some teachers "actually sought medical aid as a result of the strain during the year."[19]

## Little Rock Suffers

The violence inside Central High was matched by eruptions of hate in the city outside. Fiery crosses blazed near the houses of black people and of whites thought to be sympathetic to them. Bullets struck Daisy Bates's home and ploughed into the car belonging to school superintendent Virgil Blossom.

In November, President Eisenhower withdrew the paratroopers from Little Rock, leaving the National Guard, still under federal control, to enforce integration. There were no more soldier escorts to classes, no more safe military vehicles to transport the African Americans to school. The Little Rock Nine now used a car pool because it was risky to walk or drive alone.

Since the National Guard soldiers came from many parts of Arkansas, most were personally opposed to integration. Some of them were the same men Elizabeth Eckford had found so threatening on the first day of school. Now, despite military orders to enforce integration, their own prejudice showed.

On a single school day, two boys of the Little Rock Nine were assaulted by six white boys who shoved them, then knocked their books from their hands to kick them across the floor. Two of the African-American girls were struck by sharpened pencils, and a black boy was kicked by white schoolmates. All this happened about ten steps away from the National Guardsmen, who made no move to halt the abuse.[20]

Later, one of the guardsmen stationed at Central High wrote a fan letter to Governor Faubus. What he

*A soldier stands guard in front of Central High after the integration finally took place, a grim reminder of continued racial tensions.*

wrote shows how some of the soldiers felt: "The Arkansas National Guard people would have gone to war . . . behind you, had you rebelled against Isenhower's order."[21] The guardsman could not spell the president's name but had no trouble writing the name of his segregationist hero, Orval Faubus.

In this atmosphere of hatred, it is no wonder that Melba Pattillo braced herself every day by silently murmuring the Lord's Prayer again and again as she climbed the three flights of stairs to reach her homeroom.[22] In spite of her fears, Melba Pattillo was determined to remain at Central High, to keep the place she was holding there through so much struggle: a place not only in school but also in the larger world beyond it. She wrote in her diary, "Please, God, make space for me."[23]

# 7

# 1957: THE YEAR OF HATRED

The Little Rock crisis spread far beyond the campus of Central High School. The residents of the Arkansas capital suffered its effects every day. The formerly relaxed atmosphere of the Arkansas capital city had changed to a climate of suspicion and tension.

A white Little Rock wife and mother wrote,

> We are afraid. Tempers are too unstrung, feelings run too high, friendships and even family relationships have been strained to the breaking point. No one really knows anymore how anyone else feels . . . even physical violence can be the price of an unwisely expressed opinion. . . . No phase of our lives is untouched.[1]

A local journalist said of the situation, "Little Rock was stunned."[2] Daisy Bates wrote, "Most of the citizens of Little Rock were stunned as they witnessed a savage rebirth of passion and racial hatred that had lain dormant since Reconstruction days."[3]

The Community Chest in Little Rock was similar to such organizations in many cities. It conducted fund drives and raised money to support local charitable and service groups such as the Red Cross and the Boy

Scouts. Community Chest efforts had always been highly successful; Little Rock citizens were generous. Now the Community Chest had to accept the withdrawal of the local chapter of the moderate pro-black Urban League because city donors were angry or afraid. That did not satisfy some people because other organizations had integrated boards of directors; others had Catholic or Jewish affiliations. The antagonism against the African-American minority seemed to overflow into other groups as well. The Community Chest fell far short of its goal. Some people claimed that it was in favor of integration. Others said it was pro-segregation. Still others claimed it was not active enough on either side.[4]

## The Struggle in the News

The violence seemed at its most senseless in the attacks on reporters covering the scene. African-American newspapermen were prime targets, but whites were not spared by the mob. The entire staff from *Life* magazine was beaten up.[5] Other newspaper writers suffered blows, insults, and smashed cameras. The reporters and photographers, who came mostly from large Northern cities, were most likely considered integrationists by the mob. The violent racists also resented all national publicity.

A different kind of attack on journalism was launched against a distinguished newspaper, the *Arkansas Gazette*. Considered Little Rock's outstanding daily for generations, from the beginning of the crisis, the paper had tried to keep its reporting fair and balanced. The *Gazette*, amid the local rage, strove to be "law and order moderate." Its publisher did not wish the "traditions" or "way of life" of the state disturbed. It had favored every attempt in the courts to prevent integration at Central High. This, in some ways, made it basically segregationist. At the same time, *Gazette* editorials demanded obedience to the law.[6]

The *Gazette*'s editor, Harry S. Ashmore, criticized Governor Orval Faubus strongly. The paper had previously supported Faubus's political ambitions. But when the governor's policy brought federal troops to Little Rock, the *Gazette* changed its mind, calling Faubus "reckless." The paper also said that Faubus and his violent followers had "undone the patient work of responsible local officials."[7]

The governor struck back with accusations against the *Gazette*. His followers began a boycott that caused the cancellation of a thousand subscriptions a day for a month. In December, at the start of the Christmas shopping season, downtown Little Rock businesses began to receive anonymous letters warning of a massive boycott against their stores if they advertised in the *Arkansas Gazette*.

The newspaper tried to defend itself, saying,

> The *Gazette* has never advocated integration. The *Gazette* has never called for the breaking down of our segregation laws. On the contrary, the *Gazette* has consistently supported every legal effort to maintain the social patterns of segregation and will continue to do so.[8]

This response did little good. Worried businesspeople canceled their advertising, costing the paper many millions of dollars over the next months.

Even when both the *Gazette* and its editor won Pulitzer prizes for outstanding journalism, it did not help. Instead, this high honor only increased rage against the paper.[9]

## A City Divided

Little Rock was becoming more and more angrily divided. On one side were the traditional racists, the followers of Governor Faubus. These people included most whites who considered themselves "working people," men who wore "blue collars" to their jobs.[10] This group looked at other whites who disagreed with them as snobbish and overeducated. Sometimes they called such people Communists. They often used the word *Communist* simply to describe anyone they regarded as immoral, un-American, unpatriotic, and dangerous. On the other side in this crisis were the city's African Americans, a small number of white liberals, and many citizens who believed in upholding the law but were afraid to be drawn into the bitterness of the racial battle. A white Little Rock resident wrote, "We live in a climate of tension and fear which must only be equaled in the police states of the world."[11]

The segregationists began the new year of 1958 with another tactic. Jim Johnson, a politician and racist from the Arkansas town of Crossett, offered an amendment to the state constitution. Under it, districts with

# Chock full o' Nuts

425 LEXINGTON AVENUE

New York 17, N. Y.

THE WHITE HOUSE

Sep 16  9 16 AM '57

RECEIVED

*RECEIVED SEP 27 1957 GENERAL FILES*

September 13, 1957

The President
The White House
Washington, D. C.

My dear Mr. President:

A few days ago I read your statement in the papers advising patience. We are wondering to whom you are referring to when you say we must be patient. It is easy for those who haven't felt the evils of a prejudiced society to urge it, but for us who as Americans have patiently waited all these years for the rights supposedly guaranteed us under our Constitution, it is not an easy task. Nevertheless, we have done it.

It appears to me now, Mr. President, that under the circumstances the prestige of your office must be exerted. A mere statement that you don't like violence is not enough. In my opinion, people the world over would hail you if you made a statement that would clearly put your office behind the efforts for civil rights. As it is now, you see what the Communist nations are doing with the material we have given them.

I am aware, Mr. President, this letter expresses a mood of frustration. It is a mood generally found among Negro Americans today and should be a matter of concern to you as it is to us.

Very respectfully yours,

*Jackie Robinson*

Jackie Robinson

JR:cc

*The impact of the integration crisis reached far beyond Little Rock. Professional baseball player Jackie Robinson, who integrated major-league baseball, expressed his views on the situation in Little Rock in this letter to President Dwight Eisenhower.*

court-ordered integrated schools could simply close their schools altogether. It sounded like preparation for a long, bitter war. This amendment, along with other segregationist measures, was passed by the state legislature with Governor Faubus's blessing.

Two weeks later, Central High School received its fifth bomb threat in six days. This time, a stick of dynamite, without a fuse, was found in the building.

## Graduation Day Approaches

The hostile world of Central High seemed to cool a little for several weeks in the spring. Then, as the end of the school year approached, tensions heated up again. Ernest Green was expected to graduate on May 25. The segregationists, however, were determined that no African American would ever hold a Central High diploma. Ernest was even more determined that he would.

Ernest described his year at Central High as "a war of nerves, like being in combat."[12] Ernest had entered Central High because he felt it would give him a fine education. No one had a better right than Ernest to the best Little Rock could offer. His family had lived in the city since before the Civil War and had gained their freedom there. From the beginning of his difficult days at Central High, Ernest had kept his courage. When he was first barred from entering, he said, "It's still my school, and I'm entitled to it."[13]

In late May, a rumor spread through Little Rock. Segregationists were offering ten thousand dollars to anyone who would shoot Ernest Green before he received a Central High School diploma. This added to the fear in Quigley Stadium, scene of the graduation on May 25. No one was allowed inside without an official invitation.

One hundred soldiers were on hand to enforce order, as were extra police, and not far away, FBI agents were scanning the crowd.[14]

Principal Matthews of Central High spoke to Ernest well ahead of the ceremony. "It will be safer if we mail your diploma," he said. "You can go home if you want."

Ernest answered, "My family came to see me graduate and I won't disappoint them."[15] Later, he said, "It's been an interesting year. I've had a course in human relations first hand."[16]

By graduation day, Ernest was used to hearing threats and warnings. He had been threatened in notes and telephone calls, and told that no black would ever earn a Central High diploma, even if it took murder to prevent it. White boys at school had tormented him to provoke a fight so he could be expelled. In the face of their taunts, Ernest had kept his self-control.

Ernest had ignored the danger throughout the school year. Now, in Quigley Stadium, he paid no attention when white students sitting near him edged their chairs farther away. It mattered little to him. This was Ernest Green's personal day of triumph.

Watching the ceremony were Daisy Bates and another special guest, Reverend Dr. Martin Luther

King, Jr., who had come from Montgomery, Alabama, to honor Ernest at his graduation.

Principal Matthews delivered a commencement speech at the ceremony. There was one quite remarkable thing about it. The speech completely ignored the only thing that had made Central High School known across the country and around the world during the last year: the violent integration struggle.

Then, the names of the graduates were called out. One by one, they went to the front of the stadium as the crowd cheered and applauded. When Ernest's name was announced, a few people clapped their hands, then the stadium fell silent as the young man rose and stepped toward the stairs.

At least one of Ernest's schoolmates had been praying that Ernest would survive this moment. The night before, Melba Pattillo had written in her diary, "Dear God, Please walk with Ernie in the graduation line at Central. Let him be safe."[17]

Now the crowd waited tensely. Was this the moment when a shot would ring out, when a hidden killer would strike?

In complete quiet, Ernest Green crossed the platform to receive the high school diploma for which he had given so much and fought so bravely. He walked proudly. He had good reason to feel pride on that important day. He thought, "I am walking not only for me, but for all nine of us."[18]

But he walked for many more than just the Little Rock Nine. Ernest Green also represented the countless

African-American students of the future who would follow in his footsteps.

Despite the threats, there was no violence that day. No shots rang out. The threats and rumors proved to be only ugly words. Ernest Green became the first African-American student to earn a diploma from Central High School.

# A DIFFERENT BATTLEGROUND

The Little Rock crisis did not end on graduation day. Both sides were determined to continue the fight, but the struggle shifted from the streets and school building. The new battleground would be the courts and legislative halls.

Only a week after Ernest Green received his diploma, school board members were back in court, trying once more to end integration. They claimed that the tension and violence at Central High School distracted students from education.

Three weeks later, federal district Judge Harry Lemley ruled that integration in Little Rock would be delayed until January 1961, a year and a half in the future. The NAACP protested, saying that justice delayed was simply justice denied. The organization vowed to continue the fight.

While the legal battles of the summer dragged on, Orval Faubus was elected to a third term in the governor's office. He said, "I stand now, and always, in opposition to integration by force, and at bayonet point."[1] But it was he, of course, who had sent the first armed guardsmen to Central High.

In August 1958, the United States Court of Appeals reversed the decision of the federal district court to delay integration. The court spoke forcefully: "the time has not come . . . when an order of a federal court must be whittled away, watered down, or shamefully withdrawn in the face of violent and unlawful acts of individual citizens. . . ."[2]

There was anger and protest in the Arkansas capitol building and quiet rejoicing in many African-American homes. The school board felt it had no choice but to continue with integration. Almost everybody in Little Rock expected that the seven African-American students still enrolled at Central would be back at the high school on September 15.

The governor and the leaders of the state legislature struck back. They passed a new law that would close all Little Rock high schools. They felt that it was better to have no public schools than to have integrated ones.[3]

That same week, two quiet but significant events happened in Little Rock. A group of white Presbyterian ministers announced its disapproval of the new law to close the schools. One day later, Mrs. Adolphine Terry, one of the most prominent white citizens of Little Rock, formed a group called the Women's Emergency Committee to Open Our Schools. Mrs. Terry, an aristocratic lady of strong and independent opinions, spoke like a duchess giving royal commands. She said, "It is evident that the men are incapable of doing anything. I have sent for the young ladies."[4] The way to open the schools, she thought, was to comply with the court orders at once.

These small efforts had no real effect on the situation in the city. But, for the first time, white residents had dared speak out. This, in time, would prove important.

## The Private School Attempt

The scheduled opening day of high school in Little Rock came and went with nearly four thousand students having no classes. There was a scramble to find alternative solutions. Governor Faubus pressed for private, segregated schools to start classes in October. A Baptist church group came to the aid of the segregationists. A private, totally segregated high school would open on church-owned premises. It would depend largely on money donated by white citizens. Later, about eight hundred teenagers were enrolled before the new school quickly ran out of money and was forced to close its doors.

That September, a Little Rock woman wrote,

> No one knows when the schools will open or if the year's work will be accredited. Over the weekend more than a hundred high school age children left the city altogether. Some have gone to other cities in other states to live with relatives. . . . They are the fortunate ones, they will have a full year's schooling. . . . Many more will be unable to finish school at all. . . . Parents are frantically seeking ways to keep their teenagers occupied.[5]

*Students at private Raney High School, which opened in 1958 after Governor Orval Faubus closed the public high schools, rally on their small campus to show their support for the governor.*

Another writer said, "The city was torn apart, its reputation damaged, its public school system nearly destroyed."[6]

At about the same time, plans were announced for a new chapter of the KKK in Little Rock. One local lady, thinking of the Klan's spooky white robes, commented that the city had become ideal for youngsters: "No school and Halloween every night! Hallelujah!"[7]

The African-American students previously enrolled at Central High looked for other ways to continue high school. Elizabeth Eckford and Thelma Mothershed began to take correspondence courses to finish their senior-year studies. Melba Pattillo, Terrence Roberts, and Gloria Ray transferred to high schools outside Arkansas. Carlotta Walls and Jefferson Thomas, like hundreds of other Little Rock students, decided to wait out the year, hoping they could one day resume classes at Central High.

Governor Faubus sought to finance private schools with tax money or through the leasing of public buildings for private purposes. He was stopped by the federal courts in every attempt.[8]

Roy Wilkins, the executive secretary of the NAACP, remained hopeful. In a speech he predicted, "Common sense will take over and Arkansas will rejoin the Union."[9]

Virgil Blossom, weary of the long desegregation battle, resigned as superintendent of schools. When he left, he gave a warning: "Little Rock was a classic example of what a community should not let extremists

*Aides to Governor Faubus (center, at microphone) and national and local news reporters crowd around Faubus's desk for a press conference.*

do to it. . . . It can happen again, somewhere, some way."[10]

Five members of the school board also resigned. Only Dale Alford, who had fought against integrating Central High, remained in office. After a new election was held, the board was made up of four segregationists and three moderates.[11]

## New Year, Old Troubles

The beginning of the year 1959 found the opponents deadlocked and the schools still closed. Governor Faubus proposed an amendment to the Arkansas Constitution that would end any state obligation to provide money to support public schools. The governor also charged that three leading administrators of Central High School had done "Everything they could to discriminate against white students."[12]

The state attorney general offered a proposal to deny any member of the NAACP a job paid from state funds. The legislature quickly approved.

In May, segregationist members of the Little Rock school board tried to fire forty-four teachers and administrators because they had shown "integrationist tendencies."[13] Leading citizens of Little Rock, who had been passive or at least mild before, suddenly rose up to stop this attack against white teachers, although not all the targeted teachers were white. The African-American faculty at Dunbar and Horace Mann schools also faced firing. The new protest group called itself STOP, which stood for "Stop This Outrageous Purge." They forced a special election, won it, and so removed the three segregationist members of the school board from office. (There were only three segregationists left. Dale Alford had resigned to run for the United States Congress as a write-in candidate. He won the seat.)

The leader of the STOP protest group addressed Governor Faubus: "Leave us alone at Little Rock and let us return to the rule of reason."[14] Perhaps a turning point had at last been reached.

The United States Supreme Court ruled that the schools must reopen and integration must go ahead. Having been defeated in the highest court in the land, this was the end of the legal train for the segregationists.

*The entire school year of 1958 to 1959 was lost for most Little Rock high school students when the state legislature closed Central (whose empty hallways are seen here) and other schools rather than integrate them.*

But there was more violence to come. In early July 1959, a few days after the court ruling, a car drove slowly past the home of L. C. and Daisy Bates. A bomb was hurled at the house. It fell short and exploded in the yard, leaving an ugly crater.[15] Fortunately, no one was hurt, but this was not the first racist bombing in Little Rock. Nor would it be the last.

## The Final Confrontation at Central High

Little Rock public high schools were reopened on August 12, 1959, a month early. That morning, protesters from all parts of Arkansas gathered on the steps of the state capitol. A crowd of several hundred shouted, "We want Faubus!" as they waved the Confederate battle flags.[16]

The governor responded with a cautious warning against violence, then left the crowd. About two hundred fifty of the most emotional protesters marched toward Central High School. It looked as though last year's mob siege of the school were going to be repeated.

That day, the high school was guarded by city police, with the fire department standing by to help. Barricades blocked the school entrance. The mob, now yelling, pushed ahead. State and Confederate banners were mixed with American flags. Signs urged, "Keep Central White," while a sound truck blasted "Dixie."

The favorite chant, so often heard in front of Central High, was shouted: "Two four six eight, We don't want to integrate."[17]

*After hearing Governor Faubus and other speakers, segregationist marchers filled High Street, now renamed Martin Luther King Jr. Boulevard, on their march to Central High School in August 1959.*

Now Little Rock had a tough new police chief, Gene Smith. He had let it be known ahead of time that he would not stand for any disorder at the school. His voice amplified by a bullhorn, he ordered the mob off the street. "Your behavior is a disgraceful matter," he told them.[18]

The mob charged the barricades and a small riot ensued. Billy clubs swung, and rowdy members of the segregationist crowd were shoved into patrol cars. Twenty-four rioters were arrested. A year earlier, the Little Rock fire department had refused to help quell the disorder at Central High School. Now, firemen turned high-pressure hoses on the crowd. That marked the end of the fight, a soggy last skirmish at Central High School.

Hoses being used to douse the segregationists was a unique incident—both in Little Rock and in the history of the civil rights movement. In the long struggle for civil rights, water was used often as a weapon in several cities, but the stream was always aimed in the other direction, at African-American protesters and their allies.

Although the rioters had given up, the bombers had not. An explosion damaged a business where the city's mayor was employed. Another wrecked the fire chief's car. The school board building was also shaken by a blast. Four bombers, dedicated racists, were soon caught by the police and convicted. Governor Faubus arranged to have three of the bombers' prison sentences reduced.[19]

Governor Orval Faubus remained in political control of Arkansas for years after Central High's crisis had ended. But even during that time, the state would continue to make progress in desegregation and civil rights for African Americans. The violence that had raged around Central High School was over at last.

# 9

# CHANGING AND HEALING

Those who were in favor of segregation took their revenge in subtle ways for their defeat at Central High. Elizabeth Eckford's mother was fired from her teaching job. Carlotta Walls's father, who worked in construction as a brick mason, now found himself blacklisted by white employers. Daisy and L. C. Bates had to close their weekly newspaper after white advertisers, under pressure from racists, withdrew their advertisements. Later, the paper did reopen.

The *Arkansas Gazette* never fully recovered from the damage it suffered during the integration struggle. After long financial troubles, it merged with its rival, the *Arkansas Democrat*.

Pulitzer prize–winning *Gazette* editor Harry Ashmore left Little Rock to write books about the South that gained wide praise. Former Mayor Woodrow Mann, who had defied Governor Faubus by appealing to President Eisenhower for help, also moved away.

Orval Faubus had achieved his political ambitions, but at a terrible price. He was elected governor of

Arkansas six times. When at last he had to leave office, he fell on hard times. For a while, he worked as a bank teller in Huntsville, Arkansas.

Faubus had become a leftover from another time, a symbol of the worst kind of racism. Former *Gazette* editor Harry Ashmore said, "Orval Faubus was a hero to the mob; the nine courageous black children he failed to keep out of Central High were heroes to the world."[1]

Over the years, Faubus "went out of his way to make up with his old enemy Daisy Bates."[2] He arranged for her to be given an Arkansas Traveler award, a state honor. In 1989, hundreds of her friends gave a dinner honoring her. Faubus spoke briefly, praising her. He said that he had never held any personal resentment toward her, and "I never detected any from her."[3]

Daisy Bates was too polite to answer on such an occasion, but she did not smile. Although, in an awkward way, Faubus had tried to make amends, he had never actually apologized for his actions in the violent battle to desegregate Central High. Bates knew that many problems really are personal and must be solved in people's hearts. She wrote, "The courts can't change how white people think about blacks. They have to change themselves."[4]

At another time, Daisy Bates, speaking of school integration, had said that "Little Rock will be the first battle."[5] The battle she predicted turned out to be a war that lasted for years and spread across the

Orval Faubus ran for governor of Arkansas so many times that the rural election workers depicted in this cartoon cannot believe he has finally retired. They think the printer of the ballot has made a mistake.

American South. Even when the worst of it ended in Little Rock, it still raged elsewhere. Central High was not fully integrated until the early 1970s. There were many battles, some of them brief but violent; others were more like prolonged sieges, fierce but quiet.

Central High School made headlines very early in the African-American struggle for school integration. Other battles, just as dangerous and even more violent, would come soon. The crisis at the University of Mississippi, centering around the enrollment of African-American James Meredith in 1962, caused even more widespread rioting than Little Rock had suffered. There, President John F. Kennedy sent United States marshals to enforce the law.

Later, in 1963 in Birmingham, Alabama, Governor George Wallace imitated Orval Faubus in trying to use National Guard troops to halt integration. Once again, United States Army troops were necessary, and again, the struggle finally ended in victory for the civil rights forces. But the integration battle in Birmingham was overshadowed by the horrible bombing of the Sixteenth Street Baptist Church, where children attending Sunday school were killed in September 1963. The city of Little Rock was, by comparison, lucky. The bombs in Little Rock had failed to explode or had exploded but caused little damage. No lives had been lost.

The Central High battle was also a milestone marking the first time that an important American crisis had been shown fully on television. This was the start of a

*Governor George Wallace (left) carried on the legacy of segregation when he refused to integrate the University of Alabama in 1963.*

new world of information, sometimes called a television culture. The television cameras showed everything: the hate-filled faces of the mob, the defenseless students, the National Guard barring the way to school. Nothing could be hidden or softened. Americans saw what was happening in their own country. Many were shocked and decided to begin working to change the situation.

During the struggle at Central High, student Melba Pattillo had written that integration was a far more difficult and complicated matter than she had first supposed.[6] In fact, it turned out to be so complicated that, in 1990, more than thirty years after the crisis, plans for further desegregation were still being argued before the courts. Different schemes of busing had been tried, school district boundaries had been redrawn, and every step had been examined and argued. No move pleased everyone. Yet in the classrooms, many goals had been reached. It was not perfect. Many people were still unhappy about the racial balance. Yet, whatever remained to be done, Little Rock's schools were at last truly integrated.

## An Anniversary and a Reunion

In 1977, the fiftieth anniversary of the construction of Central High School was celebrated. Students and teachers at the school wrote a short history of Central High to give to guests. They said, "1957 is the year for which Central High School will always be remembered. This was the year which made Central High

*For a time in the 1960s, Little Rock students were taken by bus to various schools to achieve even more integration. Those enrolling today (seen here) are given wide and varied choices.*

School and Little Rock, Arkansas, symbols throughout the world of hatred, bigotry, and racial oppression."[7] The publishing of such blunt but truthful words showed how much progress had been made at the school and in the city.

In 1987, thirty years after the crisis, a headline appeared in the *Arkansas Gazette*:

THE LITTLE ROCK NINE COME TOGETHER
FOR THE FIRST TIME SINCE '57.[8]

It was a reunion worth the attention of newspaper readers. Arkansas Governor Bill Clinton, who would later become president of the United States, greeted the former students with an extended hand and a welcoming smile.

This was more than a reunion. It was a celebration of thirty years of slow but steady progress of race relations in Little Rock.

The Little Rock Nine were still famous. Reporters surrounded them, taking pictures and asking questions. A reporter called out, "How does it feel to be in Little Rock again?"

"Weird," replied Melba Pattillo.[9]

Perhaps it felt strange. Yet for all of them this was a joyful occasion. They stayed up late that night, talking and sharing memories and laughter.

This was a far different group from the frightened youngsters who had once entered Central High with mixed feelings of dread and determination. The Nine had done well in life since leaving Central High. All had been admitted to college, some earning advanced degrees. At the time they attended the reunion, Thelma Mothershed was a teacher in Illinois. Terrence Roberts had earned a doctoral degree and was a professor at the University of California, Los Angeles. Two of the Nine had become citizens of other countries: Minnijean Brown was a Canadian who lived on a farm with her six children, and Gloria Ray was now the publisher of a magazine in the Netherlands. Melba Pattillo had written books and was a resident of San Francisco. Jefferson Thomas, now of Ohio, worked as an accountant for the Defense Department. Carlotta

Walls found a successful career in real estate in Denver, Colorado. Only one of the Little Rock Nine chose to remain in Arkansas: Elizabeth Eckford first served in the United States Army. Later, she became a Little Rock probation officer. Ernest Green, after his tense graduation from Central, won a full scholarship to Michigan State University, then served as President Jimmy Carter's assistant secretary of labor for employment and training. He became a managing director of the public finance division of Lehman Brothers, a major investment banking firm. In 1987, the year of the reunion of the Little Rock Nine, Ernest Green gave the main speech at the Central High School commencement exercises. The applause and cheering he received were a far different reception from the angry silence he had faced in 1958 at his own graduation ceremonies.

A visitor to Little Rock today will find Central High School looking much as it did at the time of the crisis. It is a handsome building surrounded by well-kept lawns and large sports fields. It is an outstanding school, racially mixed, both students and faculty. Some of its principals and student-body presidents have been African Americans. The school is proud of an outstanding record of producing National Merit Scholars and fine programs in athletics, music, and the arts.

Across the street is what appears to be a well preserved, colorful vintage gasoline station. Actually, this is the Central High School Museum and Visitor

Center in the restored site of the service station that stood facing Central High in 1957.

Inside this welcoming place is a fascinating display of information and recollections of Central High School and the desegregation crisis. The museum traces the progress of school integration and civil rights in a clear and dramatic way. This center has gained wide attention and won major awards for excellence. Thousands of visitors from all parts of the country come here every year.

*Little Rock's Central High School, as it looks today.*

*This colorful gasoline station stood across from Central High during the integration crisis. Now it is the site of the Central High School Museum and Visitor Center.*

## A National Historic Site

In 1998, Central High School was named a national historic site by the United States Congress, a rare honor. President Bill Clinton greeted most of the Little Rock Nine at a White House ceremony marking the event.

First Lady Hillary Rodham Clinton recalled watching the Little Rock events as a girl in Chicago. She repeated the words of Melba Pattillo when she described the determination of the nine students to "cross the threshold into a place where angry segregationist mobs

*Arkansas Governor Bill Clinton (center) and his wife, Hillary Rodham Clinton (fifth from left), joined the 1987 celebrations remembering the integration of Central High. Bill Clinton would attend Washington ceremonies for the school's selection as a national historic site in 1998, but that time, as United States president.*

had forbidden us to go." Mrs. Clinton said, "And they did. They did it not only for themselves but for every child in America."[10]

The president also spoke to the group, saying,

> While children may never fully understand what those nine students faced as they sought to enter Central High in 1957, they do need to know what happened. . . . For all time to come, children will have an opportunity to walk the stairs you nine walked . . . to learn of your sacrifice.[11]

Ernest Green, standing near the president, looked around at the crowd gathered in the vast white tent on the White House lawn. He began, "None of us expected this to occur in September of 1957." Then he spoke for himself, for his schoolmates, their families, and for all who had helped in the struggle. He said, "We simply thought we were doing the right thing."[12]

# ★ TIMELINE ★

**1896**—In *Plessy* v. *Ferguson*, the Supreme Court rules that racially separate facilities are not unconstitutional, establishing the "separate but equal" policy.

**1954**—In *Brown* v. *Board of Education*, the United States Supreme Court ends segregation in American public schools, declaring "separate" to be always unequal in education.

**1955**—The United States Supreme Court orders integration to move ahead with "all deliberate speed."

**1956**—*January 23*: Twenty-seven African-American students are turned away when they attempt to enroll in white Little Rock schools.
*February 8*: United States district court is asked by the NAACP to require total desegregation of Little Rock schools at once; The NAACP appeals when the petition is denied.

**1957**—Segregationist groups and politicians increase their activities in Little Rock.
*August 30*: Federal Judge Ronald Davies orders the integration and opening of Central High on September 3, 1957.
*September 2*: Governor Orval Faubus orders Arkansas National Guard to stop nine black students from entering Central High.

*September 4*: African-American students turned away from Central by National Guardsmen; Elizabeth Eckford taunted by mob.

*September 20*: Governor Faubus is legally ordered to remove the Arkansas National Guard from Central High.

*September 23*: Police protection enables Little Rock Nine to enter Central, but they are removed at noon.

*September 24*: The United States 101st Airborne is sent to Little Rock by order of President Eisenhower; The soldiers will remain until November.

*September 25*: The Little Rock Nine enter Central High.

**1958**—*February 17*: Minnijean Brown is expelled from Central.

*May 25*: Ernest Green becomes the first black student to graduate from Central.

*September 14*: Governor Faubus signs a bill to close public high schools.

**1959**—*June 18*: School closing laws are ruled illegal.

*August 12*: Little Rock public high schools reopen, officially integrated; More complete integration is achieved gradually during the next several years.

**1998**—United States Congress names Central High a national historic site.

# ★ CHAPTER NOTES ★

### Chapter 1. Elizabeth Eckford Arrives at School

1. Elizabeth Huckaby, *Crisis at Central High* (Baton Rouge: Lousiana State University Press, 1980), p. 16.

2. Daisy Bates, *The Long Shadow of Little Rock: A Memoir* (New York: David McKay, 1962), p. 56.

3. *Arkansas Gazette*, September 5, 1957.

4. Bates, p. 70.

5. Ibid.

6. *The New York Times*, September 12, 1957.

7. Bates, p. 42.

8. Ibid., p. 72.

### Chapter 2. "Separate Is Unequal"

1. Charles A. Beard and Mary R. Beard, *The Rise of American Civilization* (New York: Macmillan, 1934), vol. 2, p. 266.

2. Ibid., p. 265.

3. Taylor Branch, *Parting the Waters: America in the King Years, 1954–63* (New York: Simon & Schuster, 1988), p. 651.

4. Beard and Beard, p. 268.

5. Melba Pattillo Beals, *Warriors Don't Cry: A Searing Memoir of the Battle to Integrate Little Rock's Central High* (New York: Washington Square Press, 1994), p. 29.

6. H. L. Mencken, *The American Language: An Inquiry Into the Development of English in the United States* (New York: Alfred A. Knopf, 1964), Supplement 1, p. 61.

7. Eric Foner and John A. Garraty, eds., *The Reader's Companion to American History* (New York: Houghton Mifflin, 1991), pp. 844–845.

8. Ibid.

9. Geoffrey R. Stone, Louis M. Seidman, Cass R. Sunstein, and Mark V. Tusnet, *Constitutional Law*, 2nd ed. (Boston: Little, Brown amd Company, 1991), p. 489.

10. Laura Miller, *Suggested Timeline of Events—Central High School Crisis* (Little Rock, Ark.: Central High School Museum, Inc., 1996), p. 1.

11. Beard and Beard, pp. 266–267.

12. Branch, p. 63.

13. Ibid., pp. 63–64.

14. Ibid., p. 63.

15. Ibid., pp. 63–64.

16. Ibid., p. 64.

17. Ibid.

18. Richard Kluger, *Simple Justice: The History of Brown v. Board of Education and Black America's Struggle for Equality* (New York: Knopf, 1976), pp. 408–409.

19. Richard H. Brisbane, *Black Activism: Racial Revolution in the United States, 1954–1970* (Valley Forge, Pa.: Judson Press, 1974), p. 23.

20. Kenneth B. Clark, *Prejudice and Your Child* (Boston: Beacon Press, 1954), p. 17.

21. Brisbane, p. 23.

22. Kluger, p. 782.

23. Branch, p. 113.

24. Henry Steele Commager, ed., *Documents of American History*, 6th ed. (New York: Appleton-Century-Crofts, Inc., 1958), vol. 2., pp. 799–801.

25. Brisbane, p. 24.

26. Roy Reed, *Faubus: The Life and Times of an American Prodigal* (Fayetteville: University of Arkansas Press, 1997), p. 186.

27. Brisbane, p. 25.

## Chapter 3. 1956: A Gathering Storm

1. Richard H. Brisbane, *Black Activism: Racial Revolution in the United States, 1954–1970* (Valley Forge, Pa.: Judson Press, 1974), p. 25.

2. Taylor Branch, *Parting the Waters: America in the King Years, 1954–63* (New York: Simon & Schuster, 1988), p. 245.

3. Laurie O'Neill, *Little Rock: The Desegregation of Central High* (Brookfield, Conn.: Millbrook Press, 1994), p. 18.

4. Ibid., p. 19.

5. Daisy Bates, *The Long Shadow of Little Rock: A Memoir* (New York: David McKay, 1962), p. 62.

6. Roy Reed, *Faubus: The Life and Times of an American Prodigal* (Fayetteville: University of Arkansas Press, 1997), p. 184.

7. Ibid., p. 170.

8. Ibid., p. 181.

9. Ibid.

10. O'Neill, pp. 22–23.

## Chapter 4. The Surrounded High School

1. Laurie O'Neill, *Little Rock: The Desegregation of Central High* (Brookfield, Conn.: Millbrook Press, 1994), p. 23.

2. Daisy Bates, *The Long Shadow of Little Rock: A Memoir* (New York: David McKay, 1962), p. 12.

3. *Arkansas Gazette*, September 7, 1957.

4. O'Neill, p. 24.

5. Daisy Bates, *The Long Shadow of Little Rock: A Memoir* (New York: David McKay, 1962), p. 57.

6. Roy Reed, *Faubus: The Life and Times of an American Prodigal* (Fayetteville: University of Arkansas Press, 1997), p. 198.

7. Bates, p. 110.

8. Reed, p. 208.

9. Bates, p. 60.

10. Reed, p. 208.

11. Ibid., p. 212.

12. Bates, p. 63.

13. Ibid., p. 66.

## Chapter 5. The Screaming Eagles Are Summoned

1. Melba Pattillo Beals, *Warriors Don't Cry: A Searing Memoir of the Battle to Integrate Little Rock's Central High* (New York: Washington Square Press, 1994), p. 39.

2. Ibid., p. 48.

3. Ibid.

4. Ibid., p. 50.

5. Laura Miller, *Suggested Timeline of Events— Central High School Crisis* (Little Rock, Ark.: Central High School Museum, Inc., 1996).

6. *Arkansas Gazette*, September 27, 1957.

7. Ibid.

8. Brooks Hayes, *A Southern Moderate Speaks* (Chapel Hill: University of North Carolina Press, 1959), p. 65.

9. Roy Reed, *Faubus: The Life and Times of an American Prodigal* (Fayetteville: University of Arkansas Press, 1997), p. 224.

10. Ibid., p. 225.

11. Ibid., p. 226.

12. *Arkansas Gazette*, September 29, 1957.

13. Wilson Record, *Little Rock, U.S.A.: Materials for Analysis* (San Francisco: Chandler Publishing, Co., 1960), pp. 59–62.

14. Relman Mori, "First Day of School in Little Rock," *Eyewitness to America: 500 Years of America in the Words of Those Who Saw It Happen*, ed. David Colbert (New York: Pantheon Books, 1997), p. 459.

15. Daisy Bates, *The Long Shadow of Little Rock: A Memoir* (New York: David McKay, 1962), p. 93.

16. Laurie O'Neill, *Little Rock: The Desegregation of Central High* (Brookfield, Conn.: Millbrook Press, 1994), p. 38.

## Chapter 6. Student Persecution

1. Wilson Record, *Little Rock, U.S.A.: Materials for Analysis* (San Francisco: Chandler Publishing Co., 1960), p. 71.

2. Melba Pattillo Beals, *Warriors Don't Cry: A Searing Memoir of the Battle to Integrate Little Rock's Central High* (New York: Washington Square Press, 1994), p. 132.

3. Ibid., p. 110.

4. Ibid., p. 111.

5. Daisy Bates, *The Long Shadow of Little Rock: A Memoir* (New York: David McKay, 1962), p. 101.

6. *The New York Times*, September 30, 1956.

7. *Arkansas Gazette*, September 29, 1956.

8. Ibid.

9. Ibid.

10. Bates, p. 114.

11. Orval Faubus, *Down from the Hills* (Little Rock: Pioneer Press, 1960), p. 118.

12. Beals, p. 121.

13. Ibid., p, 220.

14. Bates, p. 119.

15. Laura Miller, *Suggested Timeline of Events— Central High School Crisis* (Little Rock, Ark.: Central High School Museum, Inc., 1996), p. 10.

16. Record, p. 118.

17. Elizabeth Huckaby, *Crisis at Central High* (Baton Rouge: Lousiana State University Press, 1980), p. 88.

18. Laurie O'Neill, *Little Rock: The Desegregation of Central High* (Brookfield, Conn.: Millbrook Press, 1994), p. 46.

19. Huckaby, p. 109.

20. Roy Reed, *Faubus: The Life and Times of an American Prodigal* (Fayetteville: University of Arkansas Press, 1997), p. 233.

21. Ibid.

22. Beals, p. 147.

23. Ibid., p. 121.

## Chapter 7. 1957: The Year of Hatred

1. Elizabeth W. Blass, *Notes on the Little Rock Crisis* (Little Rock, Ark.: Unpublished manuscript, 1957), p. 1.

2. Robert S. McCord, *Central High* (North Little Rock, Ark.: Unpublished manuscript, 1998), p. 6.

3. Daisy Bates, *The Long Shadow of Little Rock: A Memoir* (New York: David McKay, 1962), p. 93.

4. Blass, p. 4.

5. McCord, p. 3.

6. *Arkansas Gazette*, October 14, 1957.

7. Ibid.

8. Ibid.

9. Roy Reed, *Faubus: The Life and Times of an American Prodigal* (Fayetteville: University of Arkansas Press, 1997), pp. 239, 242.

10. Harry Ashmore, *Arkansas: A History* (New York: W. W. Norton, 1978), pp. 281–282.

11. Blass, p. 2.

12. Laurie O'Neill, *Little Rock: The Desegregation of Central High* (Brookfield, Conn.: Millbrook Press, 1994), p. 49.

13. Alan Burns, "A Graduate in Human Relations," *Life*, June 1958, p. 109.

14. O'Neill, p. 47.

15. Ibid.

16. Burns, p. 108.

17. Melba Pattillo Beals, *Warriors Don't Cry: A Searing Memoir of the Battle to Integrate Little Rock's Central High* (New York: Washington Square Press, 1994), p. 287.

18. O'Neill, p. 50.

## Chapter 8. A Different Battleground

1. Wilson Record, *Little Rock, U.S.A.: Materials for Analysis* (San Francisco: Chandler Publishing Co., 1960), p. 104.

2. Ibid., p. 109.

3. Roy Reed, *Faubus: The Life and Times of an American Prodigal* (Fayetteville: University of Arkansas Press, 1997), p. 245.

4. Harry Ashmore, *Arkansas: A History* (New York: W. W. Norton, 1978), p. 281.

5. Elizabeth W. Blass, *Notes on the Little Rock Crisis*, Unpublished manuscript, 1957, p. 11.

6. Robert S. McCord, *Central High*, Unpublished manuscript, 1998, p. 8.

7. Blass, p. 10.

8. Reed, p. 246.

9. Record, p. 246.

10. Virgil Blossom, *It Has Happened Here* (New York: Harper & Brothers, 1959), p. 64.

11. Reed, p. 246.

12. Record, p. 138.

13. Ibid., p. 147.

14. Elizabeth Huckaby, *Crisis at Central High* (Baton Rouge: Louisiana State University Press, 1980), p. 147.

15. Daisy Bates, *The Long Shadow of Little Rock: A Memoir* (New York: David McKay, 1962), p. 162.

16. Ibid., p. 164.

17. Record, p. 166.

18. Ibid.

19. Reed, p. 257.

## Chapter 9. Changing and Healing

1. Harry S. Ashmore, *Hearts and Minds: The Anatomy of Racism from Roosevelt to Reagan* (New York: McGraw-Hill, 1982), p. 267.

2. Roy Reed, *Faubus: The Life and Times of an American Prodigal* (Fayetteville: University of Arkansas Press, 1997), p. 345.

3. Ibid., p. 245.

4. Laurie O'Neill, *Little Rock: The Desegregation of Central High* (Brookfield, Conn.: Millbrook Press, 1994), p. 57.

5. *Arkansas Gazette*, October 23, 1987.

6. Melba Pattillo Beals, *Warriors Don't Cry: A Searing Memoir of the Battle to Integrate Little Rock's Central High* (New York: Washington Square Press, 1994), p. 2.

7. *Arkansas Democrat-Gazette*, November 7, 1998.

8. Beals, p. xix.

9. Ibid., p. xx.

10. *Arkansas Democrat-Gazette,* November 7, 1998.

11. Ibid.

12. Ibid.

# ★ FURTHER READING ★

Beals, Melba Pattillo. *Warriors Don't Cry: A Searing Memoir of the Battle to Integrate Little Rock's Central High*. New York: Washington Square Press, 1995.

Fireside, Harvey, and Sarah C. Fuller. *Brown v. Board of Education: Equal Schooling for All*. Hillside, N.J.: Enslow Publishers, Inc., 1994.

Fremon, David K. *The Jim Crow Laws and Racism in American History*. Berkeley Heights, N.J.: Enslow Publishers, Inc., 2000.

Newton, Michael, and Judy Ann Newton. *Racial and Religious Violence in America*. New York: Garland Publishing Co., 1991.

O'Neill, Laurie. *Little Rock: The Desegregation of Central High*. Brookfield, Conn.: Millbrook Press, 1994.

Williams, Juan. *Eyes on the Prize*. New York: Viking Penguin Inc., 1987.

# ★ INTERNET ADDRESSES ★

Department of State. "Little Rock." *International Information Programs*. n.d. <http://usinfo.state.gov/usa/blackhis/ltrock/ltrock.htm>.

National Archives and Records Administration. "Documents Related to *Brown v. Board of Education*." *The Constitution Community*. August 2, 1999. <http://www.nara.gov/education/cc/brown.html>.

The New York Times Company. "Little Rock: 40 Years Later." *The New York Times Learning Network*. 1997. <http://www.nytimes.com/learning/general/specials/littlerock/little-rock-home.html>.

Rains, Craig. *Little Rock Central High 40th Anniversary*. 2000. <http://www.centralhigh57.org/>.

University of Arkansas Libraries. *Orval Eugene Faubus, 1910–1994*. n.d. <http://www.uark.edu/libinfo/speccoll/faubusaids/1faubusintro.html>.

White House Historical Association. "Dwight D. Eisenhower." *The Presidents*. n.d. <http://www.whitehouse.gov/history/presidents/de34.html>

# ★ INDEX ★